DAKOTA COUNTY LIBRARY
1340 WESCOTT
EAGAN, MN 55123

W9-BLK-294

HOW
TO
LIVE

also by Henry Alford

*Big Kiss: One Actor's Desperate Attempt
to Claw His Way to the Top*

*Municipal Bondage: One Man's Anxiety-Producing
Adventures in the Big City*

HOW
TO
LIVE

A Search for Wisdom
from Old People
(While They Are Still
on This Earth)

Henry Alford

NEW YORK  BOSTON

TWELVE

Copyright © 2009 by Henry Alford

All rights reserved. Except as permitted under the U.S. Copyright Act of 1976,
no part of this publication may be reproduced, distributed, or transmitted in
any form or by any means, or stored in a database or retrieval system,
without the prior written permission of the publisher.

Excerpt on page 200 from "Little Gidding" in FOUR QUARTETS, copyright 1942
by T.S. Eliot and renewed 1970 by Esme Valerie Eliot, reprinted by permission
of Houghton Mifflin Harcourt Publishing Company.

Excerpt on page 200 from "Burnt Norton" in FOUR QUARTETS by T.S. Eliot,
copyright 1936 by Houghton Mifflin Harcourt Company and renewed 1964
by T.S.Eliot, reprinted by permission of the publisher.

Excerpt on page 213 from "East Coker" in FOUR QUARTETS, copyright 1940 by
T.S. Eliot and renewed 1968 by Esme Valerie Eliot, reprinted by permission
of Houghton Mifflin Harcourt Publishing Company.

Twelve
Hachette Book Group
237 Park Avenue
New York, NY 10017

Visit our Web site at www.HachetteBookGroup.com.

Twelve is an imprint of Grand Central Publishing.
The Twelve name and logo are trademarks of Hachette Book Group, Inc.

Printed in the United States of America

First Edition: January 2009
10 9 8 7 6 5 4 3 2 1

Library of Congress Cataloging-in-Publication Data
Alford, Henry, 1962–
    How to live : a search for wisdom from old people (while they are still on this
earth) / Henry Alford.—1st ed.
        p. cm.
    ISBN-13: 978-0-446-19603-1
    ISBN-10: 0-446-19603-7
    1. Older people—Interviews. 2. Older people—Attitudes. 3. Wisdom.
4. Experience. 5. Older people—Biography. 6. Old age—Psychological aspects.
7. Older people—Psychology. 8. Aging—Psychological aspects. I. Title.
    HQ1061.A52 2009
    155.67—dc22

                                                                    2008015576

PART ONE

{ 1. }

It is commonly said—but I believe it anyway—that old people are wise. I don't mean that anyone who hits the age of seventy or so suddenly starts speaking in haiku or engaging in the kind of hyperextended, meaning-drenched eye contact that makes you look nervously down at the floor in search of a dog to pet.

No. Rather, I think that the older we get, the more life experiences we are likely to have—and the more experiences we have, the greater the body of information we have to work from. I happen to think that there are some very wise thirty-year-olds out there in the world, too—but the chances of an eighty-year-old's knowing something important about life are much greater.

We humans are one of the few species with an average life span that extends beyond the age at which we can procreate.

Why is this?

Maybe it's because old folks have something else to offer.

———

EVERY YEAR OR SO, I have an epiphany about some aspect of life. Usually, these insights are small. Take, for instance, the one I had a few years back, after buying a lot of food for a breakfast I was making for some friends. Having carefully selected an assortment of bagels, which I then gingerly placed into a brown paper bag, I was struck, two hours later, by a very, very, very profound realization: a bag of assorted bagels with one garlic bagel in it is a bag of garlic bagels.

But sometimes my insights are larger. Sometimes they reveal to me truisms about life or people and compel me to sit up and take notice. (And "truisms about life or people" is, in this instance, what I'm talking about when I say "wisdom." I'm not talking about quantum theory or knowledge comprehensible only by experts.) When this knowledge is of a universal nature, it almost unavoidably verges on being clichéd—take my realization, after a long and difficult friendship with a strikingly candid friend whose bald assertions often hurt my and others' feelings, that our greatest strengths (her candor) are usually our greatest liabilities (her candor).

When this knowledge is of a more personal nature, it can hit you with all the subtlety of a gong—like my discovery, once I'd determined that neither my crush-inducing cinema-studies professor nor my charismatic boss at my first job nor the attractive young intern I trained at that job reciprocated my affections, that most crushes are narcissistic. Their engine is flattery.

———

BUT THERE'S ANOTHER KIND OF WISDOM, too—the ability to predict the consequences of certain actions. This kind of knowledge is even more hard-won, forged as it is in the crucible of failure. And, unlike truisms about life and people, which are sometimes articulated by the young, the ability to predict consequences is almost necessarily a function of advanced years: to know that A, when followed by B, leads to C, is to have seen A and B in some rather compromised situations, very possibly at 2:00 a.m. in their underpants, in front of the kitchen sink.

This ability to predict consequences does not operate without effort. Sherwin Nuland, the clinical professor of surgery at Yale who wrote *How We Die*, writes in *The Art of Aging*, "Man is the only animal to have been granted the ability to continue developing during the later periods of life, and much of this depends on seeing oneself as the kind of person who can overcome the tendency to do otherwise."

As songwriter Eubie Blake, who lived to ninety-six, said, "If I'd known I was going to live this long, I would have taken better care of myself."

———

FOLLOWING MY LINE OF LOGIC about aging and insights, you might think that I believe that a typical ninety-year-old is twice as wise as a typical forty-five-year-old. I don't. I don't because we humans tend to forget things. We must account for attrition—valuable information is slipping through the cracks in the wall and seeping into the bed linens and evaporating into the current Boca Raton weather system.

But maybe I can catch and curate some of it before it slips off into the night.

———

WISDOM IS SLIPPERY. It comes in many forms and guises. Sometimes it is intermingled with a certain amount of *un*wisdom.

But however difficult wisdom can be to pin down, one thing is certain: the curtains don't come crashing down when you hit seventy. In fact, the years after "threescore and ten"—the decade that Psalms 90 tells us is the span of our lives because anything after eighty "is only labor and sorrow"—are a ripe time for realizations and breakthroughs. The reasons for this are varied. For some people, retirement finally gives them the time to contemplate their navels. Some come to conclusions as a result of their or others' increasing proximity to the end. Cicero wrote in 44 B.C., "Since [nature] has fitly planned the other acts of life's drama, it is not likely that she has neglected the final act as if she were a careless playwright."

We tend to think of life after seventy—outside of medical ailments, of course—as being soft and muzzy and fairly static: lots of cardigan sweaters and an increasingly housebound devotion to a small, irritable pet. But for many people, it's anything but. Grandma Moses started painting in her seventies; Michelangelo finished sculpting the Rondanini Pietà when he was nearly ninety. Benjamin Franklin helped frame the U.S. Constitution at eighty-one; Golda Meir assumed leadership of Israel at seventy, and Nelson Mandela assumed leadership of South Africa at seventy-six.

Others aren't starting new projects or professions or life situations but are altering their involvement with professions or life situations they've been in for years—rethinking their marriage, changing how they write or paint, deciding never ever again to tolerate anyone who calls them "Dollface." In 2006, *Newsweek* ran a story about how eighty-seven-year-old preacher Billy Graham, who'd spent most of his adult working life in the spotlight, had in his old age shifted his animus from partisan politics to the purely heavenly. The former political gadabout now refused to offer either an opinion on stem-cell research or counsel to world leaders. He told the magazine, "The older I get, the more important the eternal becomes to me personally."

Whatever the realizations are that these older folks make—and whether these realizations apply only to themselves or have a more universal nature—it's safe to say that these mental breakthroughs are not always easily won and that the paths that lead to them are sometimes full of misdirection. As with any creative process, there is often a period of doubt and mental thrashing.

Over the years, I've seen my mother, now eighty, grapple

with questions about her life in ways that seem specific to her age. I remember lying on a Caribbean beach with her two years ago when she said, "Let me talk about Will. I want to know what you think my obligations to him are."

I'd taken her along with me on a glamorous travel-writing assignment, which had necessitated her leaving behind Will, whom she'd lived with for thirty-one years, twenty-three of them as his wife.

My mother and stepfather, it seems, had taken different approaches to aging. Mom was increasingly out of the house, more eager than ever to create a whirlwind of travel and painting classes and rug hooking and fun, while Will had grown increasingly morose and sedentary. He was still a voracious reader—Will has been known to polish off three books in a week—but he was increasingly bedroom bound. As my brother once put it, "Will sleeps fourteen hours a day. He's like a male lion."

I asked Mom if she felt guilty coming on the trip with me; she said no, Will had always been very supportive of her travels. But she worried that his life had become so small—semiretired, he'd resigned from the local historical committee and from the town board in the small central Massachusetts town they lived in. She said, "His only activity besides napping and reading and watching TV is going to get the mail."

"Well," I said, trying to put a nice spin on it, "at least his situation is self-created. It's not like you're running off to the Caribbean while he has a fatal disease."

"True," she said, reaching into her bag for some suntan lotion.

"Do you miss him?" I asked.

"Not really. Isn't that awful?"

"Did you use to miss him when you traveled?"

"Yes. But I have a thick shell now."

I pointed out, "He's sort of gotten harder to love as he's gotten older."

"Yes," she said. "And maybe my thick shell is my fear of losing him."

The heart wants what it wants, especially in later life. But what if the heart hasn't yet made up its mind?

———

THE FACT—or should I say, cliché—that old people are wise is not merely rooted in anecdotal evidence. There's medical evidence, too. Until the 1970s or so, the mind was considered merely to be part of the brain and not part of one's biological being. Recent studies in neuroscience, however, show that the brain has a powerful ability to influence its own aging. Nuland explains in *The Art of Aging* that "it is no longer enough to conceive of the mind as a function only of the brain; it must be thought of as influenced by the very factors that it has long been recognized to influence, namely the body and our perception of the environment in which we find ourselves." Although we experience a 5 percent or so decrease in brain weight and volume every decade after we reach forty, the actual number of brain cells in healthy older people decreases only marginally. From a neurological point of view, it takes us longer to learn things as we grow older and older, and our creative thinking, short-term memory, and problem-solving abilities dwindle, but, Nuland writes, "the ability to assimilate information and to learn from the experience does not change appreciably."

And according to some, that ability actually improves. In his book *The Wisdom Paradox*, Elkhonon Goldberg, a clinical professor of neurology at the New York University School of Medicine, writes that, as we age, we get better and better at pattern recognition. According to Goldberg, "we accumulate an increasing number of cognitive templates," so that "decision-making takes the form of pattern recognition rather than of problem-solving."

The basis of this pattern recognition is so-called generic memories. Goldberg gives an example: say you're unsuccessfully trying to come up with someone's name. But then, as soon as the person walks into the room, you suddenly remember it. In order for this to happen, your brain must have housed a network that contained both a visual component (the face) and an auditory component (the name). Goldberg writes, "Despite the fact that these two kinds of information inhabit very different cortical areas (the parietal lobe for facial information and the temporal lobe for name information) they are intertwined in a single attractor." He concludes, "This, in a nutshell, is the mechanism of generic memory."

Goldberg illustrates the importance and power of this decades-tested intuition in a very unusual way. He points to the various forms of brain disease evidenced in the leaders of the twentieth century—Reagan's Alzheimer's, Hitler's memory decline and Parkinson's, Stalin's and Lenin's multi-infarct diseases, Mao's ALS, Churchill's and Thatcher's series of strokes, Brezhnev's senility. "What allowed these remarkable personalities to prevail despite neurological decline," Goldberg writes, "was the rich, previously developed pattern-recognition facility, which enabled them to tackle a wide range of new situations, problems and challenges, as if they were familiar ones."

I'm no neurologist, but I can certainly attest to my own increased powers, even at the modest age of forty-five, of intuition. For instance, I've gotten much better over the years at immediately gauging which of the acquaintances I make will become longtime friends; and I now know that any movie trailer that features a lot of extreme close-ups of a fountain pen skritching along a piece of paper is an ad for a movie that is going to view The Life of the Writer with a kind of gauzy romanticism that will make me feel like I've crossed the Atlantic in a rowboat.

The paradox inherent in our increased ability to recognize

patterns, of course, is that it occurs simultaneously with large amounts of memory loss. And it is this memory loss that I hope will give my quest a special urgency. If people are repositories of knowledge—the death of an old person, an African saying runs, is like the burning of a library—then I want a library card. I want borrowing privileges for the rest of my life.

As if this attitude weren't self-serving enough, there's an even more selfish element to my quest, too. Namely, I hope to get a preview of my own old age. Having three older siblings—the eldest, my sister Kendy, is thirteen years older than I—has been a boon to me because I have constantly been served examples of what lay, or did not lie, before me. Maybe my interactions with older folks will provide a similar forecast. If you know the advantages and disadvantages of a destination before you reach it, you can sometimes savor or extend the former and delay or thwart the latter. Leonardo da Vinci once wrote, "If you are mindful that old age has wisdom for its food, you will so exert yourself in youth, that your old age will not lack sustenance."

Like many people, I have a strange relationship with aging. When I started getting gray hairs at the age of forty-three, I spent two years carefully cutting them from my temples; but I'm also someone who would never choose to live in a new building and who will sometimes wash a new shirt ten or eleven times before wearing it for the first time. Why do I want everything around me to be old while laboring under the misconception that I myself am ever youthful? I see the changes that life visits upon me—I used to be svelte, but with age I have svelled—and wonder, Am I ready for what's ahead?

And so I have decided to interview and spend time with as many fascinating senior citizens as I can. I will ask them about their dawning realizations, and I will ask them what they've learned, and I will ask them, the next time I'm putting together a picnic, whether I should be putting the one garlic bagel in its own biocontainment bag.

A word about this book's title. I in no way mean to suggest by it that I myself am proposing a way for others to live. Rather, I am the listener here; it is my interviewees who I hope will be making all the recommendations.

Mark Twain once said, "Wisdom is the reward you get for a lifetime of listening when you would rather have talked."

And, oh, how some oldsters can *talk*.

I 'll sit here," she said, hunkering her tiny, slightly stooped body down onto her bed, which seemed to take up about a fourth of her bedroom. Pointing at a canister-style respirator on the floor, she explained, "I have this at night. It keeps your brain."

I could hear the emphysema in her voice.

I smiled awkwardly and sat in a chair near her desk.

"I'm so honored to meet you," I said, my genuine enthusiasm colored only by my surprise that a woman of her advanced years would, having only swapped three or four phone messages and e-mails with him, let a total stranger into her house and then bring him into her bedroom.

"Thank you, that's very kind," she said. "It's all age, you know."

"What do you mean?"

"Anyone could have done what I did. But I was eighty-nine then . . ."

She directed her gaze somewhere in the mid-distance, momentarily lost in thought. When she reconnected her line of vision with mine, a look of Yankee defiance came across her face: "I'm ninety-seven now."

ON THE FIRST DAY of 1999, Doris Haddock, a.k.a. Granny D, set off on a fourteen-month, 3,200-mile walk across the country in support of campaign-finance reform. In addition to the emphysema she had contracted after fifty years of cigarette smoking, she had severe arthritis in her hands and knees. She wore hearing aids. She had dentures. She was not, in short, what you'd call Olympics-ready.

The passing of the McCain-Feingold bill and its limiting of lobby-based or "soft" campaign financing was her chief goal. In support of the cause, Granny D gave speeches and interviews as she traversed the nation, and she had people she met along the way sign a petition reading, "We, the people of the United States of America, beseech our leaders to enact, with all speed, campaign finace reform, eliminating 'soft money' from political campaigns."

But she had a more personal impetus for turning herself into a human stunt puppet, too. She hoped to console her grief over the death of her husband and her best friend, Elizabeth, who had died within a year of each other, six years earlier. She felt like she'd never properly grieved Elizabeth's death. Several times during her walk, she cried herself to sleep thinking about her friend.

———

GRANNY D dropped out of college during the Depression to support her family. She worked for twenty years at a factory in Manchester, New Hampshire, the town where many presidential campaigns bloom or wither. Then, in the early eighties, after she'd retired with her husband to a small town near Peterborough, Granny D nursed him through ten years of Alzheimer's. He passed away in 1993. They had been married for sixty-two years.

"Now that Elizabeth and my husband no longer needed me," Granny D writes in her eponymous book, published in 2001, "I had been worrying about how I might use what remained of my own time."

When the McCain-Feingold bill was first quashed in the Senate in 1995, Granny D got vocal. She ranted to her Tuesday Morning Academy, a group of women who meet for conversation and activities, telling them, "You can't get elected unless you have a million dollars." Granny D and some of the academy members put together a petition and sent it off to New Hampshire's two senators; one replied with a form letter saying that spending money was a form of political speech, and the other didn't respond at all.

"That wonderful feeling of belonging, of being a valued participant, was jerked away," Granny D writes. "I fully understood: I was no longer a village elder at the council fire. I was a woman scorned."

The sparks hit the tinder one February afternoon. Having just returned from her best friend's funeral, Granny D told *Yankee* magazine, she was driving through the Florida Everglades with her son, Jim, when they saw an old man walking on the side of the road, carrying only a paper bag. He was miles from any town or house. He leaned on his cane and blew his nose with his bare fingers. Granny D asked Jim, "What on earth do you suppose he's doing?"

"Well, Ma, it looks like he is on the road," Jim said.

"You mean, on the road like Willie Nelson?"

"Yes."

"Or like Jack Kerouac?"

"Yes."

Intrigued, Granny D asked Jim if he had ever wanted to walk across the country.

"Well, yes. But I have to earn a living," he said. "And you're too damn old."

"Says who?"

Pity the man who underestimates the righteous.

———

TODAY, a brisk, sunshiny day in 2007, my first sighting of the activist-phenom took place in her driveway. When she'd heard my rental car crunching along the gravel, she came out and stood in front of her house. She was anxiously rubbing her thumb along the pad of her fingers.

Five feet tall and apple-cheeked, Granny D exudes a kind of New England–style wholesome fierceness; if you saw her standing behind the counter of a country store, you'd know that her shopkeeping ethics are scrupulous and that her chocolate-chip cookies have exactly the right amount of salt. She lives now with her son, Jim, in a dark, unfinished house on a heavily wooded road outside Peterborough, one of the towns Thornton Wilder made famous in *Our Town*. She lives on Social Security.

"I've been waiting five minutes!" she greeted me, not without irritation. I apologized. She gave me a flinty smile and said, "Never mind." Taking my wrist in her hand, she led me into the house, to her bedroom. She was casually dressed in slacks but had a colorful silk scarf wrapped around her neck.

Once she'd sat on her bed, she pointed to the phone sitting on the desk to my right and said, "I'm waiting for an important call." She was waiting for someone to sign his name to an op-ed piece about her new cause, voluntary public funding. Under voluntary public funding, or clean elections—now in operation in seven states and two cities—a politician must first collect a threshold sum of small contributions, to show community support (and dissuade carpetbaggers); then he gets a grant but forswears all private funding. New Hampshire was going to vote on instituting voluntary public funding four months hence. She told me, "My vision is that if a sufficient number of states accept it, a critical mass will form. A great many of our laws are passed that way. If it passes and we're federally funded"—here she switched to a theatrical stage whisper—"*we'll change the world*."

"Well, if your phone call comes in, please don't not answer it on my account," I said.

"Oh, I won't," she said, chuckling.

———

I'D GOTTEN IN TOUCH with Granny D after seeing a documentary about her called *Run Granny Run*, which is less about her walk than about one of her subsequent political efforts—her unsuccessful 2004 run for Senate against the popular New Hampshire senator Judd Gregg. The film captures the grueling rigors of campaigning, particularly for a candidate who refuses all PAC money. When two shots in the movie made my eyes well with tears—both are of the widow praying bedside; she is on her knees, wearing tube socks, and the high angle of the camera makes a banquet of her humility—I knew I wanted to try to talk to her. I got in touch with Ruth Meyers, one of Granny D's squad of volunteers. Meyers explained that Granny D was currently extremely busy with her current mission: "A while back, Doris said, 'There's one more thing I'd like to see before I lay down my head. I'd like to see the public funding bill for campaign financing reform passed.'" And so began a whirlwind of personal appearances and activism.

Granny D's bedroom was dark and filled with memorabilia; a three-legged German shepherd mix huddled comfortably on the floor next to Granny D's respirator. I started, "You've said that the key to a happy life, especially in one's later years, is to help other people until you don't notice your own needs and pains anymore."

"It's true," she told me, repositioning a pillow behind her back. "It's something bigger than yourself."

"And why does that help?"

"Well, do you realize what could happen? Do you realize that I'm saving the world?" She smiled here, seemingly amused at the brazenness of her statement, and continued, "Come on—it's possible! It's like a mouse with a big cheese. You start with a little bit, and then a little bit, and then a little bit, and pretty soon the cheese is gone, and you've done it. It's only little triumphs that keep you going."

"And then you try to stack them up into one big one?" I surmised.

"Exactly."

That's certainly a philosophy that would get a walker all the way across the country. When Granny D first told her family about her plan, her sister cried, and her son-in-law suggested that Granny D was a candidate for institutionalization. But onward Granny D trod, walking through 208 towns in thirteen states; she outlasted four pairs of sneakers, four sun hats, three support vans, and three managers. Each day, after she'd walked ten miles, she would spray-paint onto the road a yellow line to denote where she should start the next day; then someone would drive her to her accommodations for the evening. She'd received few responses when she'd written letters to local police stations and houses of worship before the trip, asking if she could sleep in their jail cells or common areas, but she ended up staying mostly with friends of friends or at the homes of like-minded volunteers or in donated motel rooms.

Starting in Pasadena, she made it without incident until the Mojave Desert, where she came down with pneumonia and dehydration and was rushed to a hospital for four days. (After this, her son and an Arizona political activist named Dennis Burke arranged to have a number of vehicles trail Granny D for the rest of the trip, including a camper she slept in. Burke later cowrote her book.)

When she revived, she kept on going—from Dalhart, Texas, to Hooker, Oklahoma, to Kismet, Kansas, to Odin, Illinois, to Versailles, Indiana, to Chillicothe, Ohio, to Clarksburg, West Virginia. Along the way, she drew into her orbit random temporary tagalongs—kids on bikes, small-town mayors, and West Virginia's octogenarian secretary of state. (Granny D writes, "I was not sure at first if his passion was for reform or for me.") She was the object of much national media attention, a fact she found flattering but somewhat baffling. "I don't know why my opinion seemed to be worth more when I was walking than when I was sitting in my living room back in New Hampshire," she wrote, "but maybe it is explained by that old saying that an expert is anyone from more than 50 miles away."

When she met with heavy snows in the Smoky Mountains, she was forced to cross-country ski; she skied the last hundred miles into Washington, D.C. There, despite having never made a public speech prior to starting on her trek fourteen months earlier, she stood on the steps of the Capitol and announced, "These houses of Congress are being turned into houses of prostitution!"

———

GRANNY D's EFFORTS drew praise and support from thousands of people, including John McCain, Bill Moyers, and Jimmy Carter. ("Very nice," Granny D said, when I asked her what it felt like to draw praise from these three. "And they still remember me, too. I can get any one of them right on the phone.") Pete Seeger said that her book "is one of half a dozen—including *Silent Spring* and *Walden* —which have turned my life around." When the McCain-Feingold bill passed in 2002, Granny D was standing in the congressional gallery. "Ohhh, that was a good feeling," she told me, her otherwise flinty expression giving way to a sly twinkle.

McCain asked Granny D to stand next to him when he announced his run for president, but she felt she had to turn him down.

"Was that a difficult decision to make?" I asked.

"It was. I felt I had walked across the country for him and that if I had faith in him I should support him. But I'm not a politician. I'm an activist. I couldn't stand next to him—I'd be supporting him. If I supported anyone, it'd be Dennis Kucinich. When I heard Kucinich speak—the power of that man! He took the earth to the moon! He was wonderful. But they say he's not electable."

"Well, he's very short," I said. "That's the shallow response. When you see him on a stage with other candidates . . ."

"He looks like a boy. A young boy."

"It's so silly that height would be a factor," I said.

"You can't be Napoléon anymore."

———

TWO MONTHS AFTER HER WALK, Granny D returned to Washington to continue banging on her proverbial drum. This time, she read the Declaration of Independence aloud under the rotunda of the Capitol, whereupon police arrested her for demonstrating, handcuffed her, and took her to the police station. A month later, when she appeared before a judge to answer the charges, she told him, "Your honor, the old woman who stands before you was arrested for reading the Declaration of Independence in America's Capitol building. I did not raise my voice to do so and I blocked no hall . . . Your honor, we would never seek to abolish our dear United States. But alter it? Yes. It is our constant intention that it should be a government of, by, and for the people, not the special interests . . . In my 90 years, this is the first time I have been arrested. I risk my good name, for I do indeed care what my neighbors think about me. But, your honor, some of us do not have much power, except to put our bodies in the way of justice—to picket, to walk, or to just stand in the way. It will not change the world overnight, but it is all we can do." The judge charged her only an administrative fee of ten dollars rather than the five hundred he could have charged her, and he praised her efforts on behalf of the "silent masses."

Granny D pointed out to me our national history of elitism, saying, "We started up with white men with property, that's who could vote." She added, "We don't have a democracy, and we never have had a democracy."

———

I KNEW FROM READING HER BOOK what Granny D attributes the success of her sixty-two-year marriage to: "great sex" and never letting the sun go down on her anger. "Call a truce," she writes. "See the humor in the situation. Make sure you think about how unimportant the issue really is in comparison to the troubles of the whole world."

But I wasn't sure what she thought the secret of her longevity and tenacity is, so I asked.

"Hmm. Well, it's not good eating," she said. "I eat what I like."

"Yes, chocolate figures large in your book," I pointed out.

A silence ensued, so I tried out a theory: "I would think that your curiosity might be your greatest life force."

"Light horse?" she asked.

"Life force."

"Oh. That I have determination."

"Yes."

"Well, I'm very stubborn. I'm very stubborn."

My mind flashed back to the moment in the Mojave Desert when Granny D realized she'd contracted pneumonia. She was having a predawn bowl of cereal when she launched into a coughing fit and suddenly couldn't breathe. Taken to a hospital, she got a call from Dennis Burke that night, who told her that it was remarkable that she'd walked from Pasadena to the Mojave, and that now she could hand over the baton to other people, who would finish the walk.

"My breath was still short," Granny D writes, "but not so short that I couldn't bark at him for such a thought. I told him that I was prepared to die as part of this journey, if need be. It would be preferable to sitting at home, wishing I had continued. We're all dying, and we might as well be spending ourselves in a good cause."

I told Granny D, "It's interesting that your philosophy of life is so service based, and yet you're not churchy in the book at all, so agnostics like me can join in the fun."

She replied, "As you get older and older, you think, Come on, this is ridiculous—do you really think there's going to be something after you go? Do you really think there's something waiting for you, heaven or hell? Come on. Let's face it. I've led a Christian life, don't get me wrong, but now it's getting to the end of time and I just know. I just know. I will go through the ceremonies but I would be very surprised if there's something waiting for me."

———

AFTER WE'D TALKED for almost two hours, both Granny D's and my energy was starting to flag. I thanked her for talking with me, and we both stood and walked out to the hallway. About six feet before the front door, I noticed a gorgeous Oriental-looking hooked rug and admired it. Granny D told me that she'd made it while she was taking care of her dying husband.

I stared down at the rug. Suddenly, it was even more transfixing to me. That she could transform this period of hardship into something so beautiful deeply impressed me. I was reminded that Pablo Picasso, on the morning that he died at age ninety-one, asked if there was a canvas that was stretched and ready to be painted.

I'd like to tell you that when I started out on my quest I had a highly defined idea of what wisdom is. But it's easier to say what wisdom *isn't*. One of the more famous examples comes from a scene in the 1967 movie *The Graduate*. Recent college graduate Benjamin Braddock (Dustin Hoffman) is buttonholed by Mr. McGuire, a friend of his father's, at a cocktail party.

> McGuire: Come on with me for a minute. I want to talk to you. I just want to say one word to you, just one word.
> Benjamin: Yes, sir.
> McGuire: Are you listening?
> Benjamin: Yes, I am.
> McGuire: *Plastics.*
> (*A pause.*)
> Benjamin: Exactly how do you mean?

What's unwise here—and I'm presuming by the laughter that the scene elicits in theaters that we agree on the lack of wisdom—is the lack of proportion and context that McGuire displays when he drops his bombshell. Plastics may indeed be a lucrative business to go into, but, as with all ventures, one should entertain some doubts and consider the possible downside—moral, environmental, aesthetic, as well as financial. But McGuire is without doubt. And, more important, who knows if Ben is even *interested* in polymers and resins?

The tricky part of wisdom is that it usually necessitates a bicameral mind-set: at its heart, wisdom is the knowledge of what is true or right or just. But it also needs a healthy sense of doubt, because without that, you're an ideologue.

Granny D has these qualities. Moreover, her rug, like her walk across the country, suggests that she's someone who can turn loss into gain. If you can turn out a beautiful rug while your husband is slipping away from you, and if you can let his subsequent death and the death of your best friend help fuel a cross-country hejira of personal and political gain, then maybe you also have a unique ability to apprehend the beauty of the tornado or the terror of the rose.

There's a passage in Granny D's book in which she talks about how her fascination with roadkill sometimes put her fellow walkers off. She saw a lot of carcasses on her trek; she came across foxes, rattlesnakes, and hummingbirds, not to mention "cracked-open armadillos and polecats." She liked to get up close and get a gander at these fatalities—"The color and texture of their innards and the expressions on their faces are worth looking at if you are not put off by death." Just outside of Phoenix, she was walking with a needy vegetarian who looks like "the Carradine boy from *Kung Fu*." The duo stumble upon a dead fox in the road. His body is still warm. The vegetarian drags the carcass under a tree. Granny D waxes philosophical, saying, "If you are afraid of death, you are afraid of life, for living your life leads to death. Until you face death and see its beauty, you will be afraid to really live—you will never properly burn the candle for fear of its end."

———

GRANNY D'S PHONE CALL finally came right then, while we were standing in her hallway, admiring her rug.

"There's my call! Say good-bye," she said excitedly, giving me a warm hug.

I drove about ten minutes to the Peterborough town library to check my e-mail before heading back to New York. Inside, I poked my head into a mostly empty office, on one of whose walls hung a poster that had caught my eye.

It read, "I was put on earth to accomplish a certain number of things and I am so far behind that I will never die."

{ 3. }

How best to canvas the world of people over seventy?

I drew up lists of names of people whom I wanted to talk to. These lists begat other lists, which in turn begat other lists. There were hundreds of folks I wanted to try to get in touch with. I wanted to talk to someone who'd recently changed his mind about something important in his life, and I wanted to talk to someone who'd overcome, or was trying to overcome, a stumbling block or crisis. I wanted to talk to people I had admired for a long time—Jimmy Carter and Phyllis Diller and Ram Dass and Edward Albee and Sandra Day O'Connor; the list went on and on. I wanted to spend some time with my friend Sandra's father, an eccentric Chinese man who takes the art of recycling to a very, very high level, including using a battered cardboard cereal box for his briefcase and eating food that he finds in garbage cans and dumpsters.

It was great fun to brainstorm for names. Sometimes they would pop into my brain, unbidden. One morning, I was foggily bumping around the apartment doing my morning routine—looking for a pair of socks; having a brief cuddle with Hot Rod, our seventeen-year-old cat; trying, for the second time in ten minutes, to find my cup of coffee—while Greg was in the midst of his own ritualized set of preparations, when we happened to cross paths in the doorway between the living room and dining room, whereupon, as if receiving instructions from outer space, I robotically uttered, "Noam Chomsky."

Once I'd assembled my lists of names, I did some weeding. I discarded the names of anyone whose own account of his or her wisdom I felt I could not improve upon or enhance (Elie Wiesel, Joan Didion, Calvin Trillin, memoirist Doris Grumbach). I removed the names of people who have been given ample opportunity to tug on their proverbial beard (the Dalai Lama) or whose affiliation to an institution might curb his or her individuality (most clergy, Senator Robert Byrd). I didn't want to talk to anyone who didn't want to talk to me, so I removed the names of the famously reclusive or press shy (J. D. Salinger, Cormac McCarthy, photographer Helen Levitt). And I stalled on, and ultimately did not contact, anyone who had committed a specific wise or inspiring act but whom I did not otherwise know enough about (Rose Morat, a 101-year-old mugging victim who fought back at her assailant; entrepreneur Lisa Gable, who launched the Strap-Mate to combat the problem of collapsing bra straps).

I sent out hundreds of e-mails, presenting myself as a journalist hot on the path of wisdom. Responses trickled back, some of them positive.

As I started to meet with people, it became immediately clear that the tenor of my encounters would often confound my expectations. For instance, I expected my interview with my teacher from second grade—Achsah Hinckley, who'd been a wonderfully inspiring and inventive teacher at the Bancroft School in Worcester, Massachusetts—to be sunny, but instead I learned what a hard life she's had. She'd been fired from the school after someone complained that she was offering voluntary prayer in her classroom; her alcoholic husband had, prior to his death in 1981, depleted her savings. As we sat in her living room and talked, I could see how intellectual rigor and a Puritan work ethic had kept the skinny, fastidious eighty-one-year-old afloat all these years, but I could also see that the float had sometimes necessarily wobbled. "I wish I'd gone to Europe for a year. I wish I'd been more daring," she told me. "But I was a Depression child, and security meant so much to me."

Conversely, I expected that the trials and vagaries of forty-seven years of performing stand-up comedy on the road would have darkened the brow of my childhood idol, Phyllis Diller. After all, she's written that her first husband was "cruel and brutal" and an "agoraphobic sex tyrant." She thinks she's so homely that she's "never made Who's Who but I'm featured in What's That?" She's so casual about getting plastic surgery—she was one of the first celebrities to cop to it—that she's gone to parties with stitches sticking out of her face or with her glasses taped to her forehead so that they wouldn't weigh heavily on her fragile new nose. ("I had to do something," Diller has said. "I was so wrinkled, I could screw my hats on.")

But when the ninety-year-old Diller granted me a phone interview, I could barely penetrate her force field of positive thinking. She told me, "When I got into the business, I gave myself the luxury of perfect focus. I looked straight ahead and did everything toward making it in the business. I never looked right, I never looked left. Never had a moment of doubt."

"Truly?" I asked. "Never a moment of doubt?"

"Never, never. I learned that that's the way to fail. My own secret was to protect myself from negativity. It can come from friends, it can come from your husband, it can come from anywhere. Mentally, I was wearing a white feather cape."

I said, "But life throws obstacles at us all the time, right? I mean, what would you do if, say, someone heckled you or talked during your routine?"

"With my act, you would have had to *make an appointment* to

talk or heckle. My timing is perfect. The thing that draws heck-
lers is silence. You would have had to *make an appointment*."

"Huh. Well, you *do* hold the Guinness world record for de-
livering twelve punchlines in a minute—"

"I do, I do, I do!" she trilled. "That's the secret. You have to
fill the air with fun!"

Cue loud, unhinged Diller-icious cackle.

———

NOT EVERYONE wanted to get on board the wisdom train.

The people who were uninterested or unable to participate
in my project fell into three categories. The first—the largest—
group was of those who responded with total silence. This, as it
turns out, is standard procedure for many people, regardless of
whether or not they are besieged by requests from the media.
Many has been the time that I've reached out to someone to say
that I'm writing a story for a one-million-or-more-circulation
publication and wonder if they have anything to contribute, only
to meet with no response whatsoever. I don't take this personally. I take this to mean that the person doesn't want to burden
me with an e-mail or phone call that bears no treat. There is a
certain politesse to the soft rejection.

The second group was made up of those people who were
unable to participate for some reason. "While Mr. Cosby ap-
preciated hearing from you," ran an e-mail I received from Norman R. Brokaw, the chairman of the William Morris Agency,
"I did want to let you know that he will not be participating in
your project; he just does not have the available time. As I'm sure
you can imagine, Mr. Cosby is continually besieged by countless
hundreds of organizations, companies, schools, and individuals
with requests similar to yours not only from this country but
from abroad as well. As much as he'd like to say yes to so many,
it's just impossible for him to comply with everyone's request.

As a result, his numerous charitable and contractual obligations over the next several years, which includes writing his own books, preclude him from taking on any additional activity than that to which he is already committed. I trust you can understand." After that disquisition, even someone as obtuse as I am can understand.

The only age-based refusal to my interview requests I received was from Don Rickles's manager, who told me, "Even though he's eighty years old, he doesn't like to talk in those terms."

I wasn't always sure how aggressive to be. Some of the folks I was interested in talking to were of an age or physical condition that demanded deference be paid them. Moreover, at times I wondered if it was worthwhile or even possible to prompt someone into being wise. There were times when I thought that maybe getting someone to be wise is like getting someone to be funny—both are, in their ideal forms, freely willed. That said, though, it's possible to put someone up to being wise—to set the trap, as it were. But it is not fruitful to badger someone into it. Lest I be guilty of passivity, though—I am semi-haunted by two sentences from psychologist Mary Pipher's book *Another Country: Navigating the Emotional Terrain of Our Elders* that runs, "Doing interviews for this book, I learned to let the phone ring fifteen times. I learned to wait at doors for five minutes after I rang the bell"—I tried to determine whether a nonresponse was the product of treatable modesty or whether it was the product of inability or disinterest. For instance, I'd called hundred-year-old cultural critic Jacques Barzun, who's famous for making the statement "Whoever wants to know the heart and mind of America had better learn baseball." *The New Yorker* had just profiled him, and Barzun had said, "Old age is like learning a new profession. And not one of your own choosing," which led me to think that he might prove a fertile interview. When Barzun did not return my call for two weeks, I called him again and pleaded my case; he told me, "I'm sorry, I have to turn down interviews. My mind is just as active, but I have difficulty speaking."

The third category of people included those who flirted or waffled. I knew, for instance that James Hillman, the archetypal psychologist and author of *The Soul's Code*, was uncomfortable with talking too much about himself. I tried to convey to him that our interview could be largely theory based. He wrote back an e-mail titled, "Possible Interview." The Possible Interview came with a Possible Date. But when I called Hillman the day before the possible date, all was Impossible. He said he'd call back. He did, a month or so later, at which point he asked me to remind him what he'd agreed to. I said a possible interview. I added that I would meet him anywhere. He suggested we talk by phone three weeks hence. I said I'd rather meet in person, but that, sure, a phone interview was better than no interview. But when I e-mailed him the day before the newly possible interview, he called back and said he wouldn't be available. He pleaded, "I have no time at all. It's a hopeless life. And I have nothing else to say! It's all in those books."

"You're very reluctant, aren't you?" I asked.

"Well, I just have so little time," he said.

He said that he'd try, sometime in the following three weeks, to "steal away" from his obligations and give me a phone call. I said I would be honored if he would do so. I still would be.

———

I ALSO BEGAN TELLING MY FRIENDS and colleagues about my quest. Most of the reactions fell between positive and dewy-eyed.

"Ooooh, I wish you could have talked to my aunt Bea," my friend Suzi said. "One time she warned me, '*Be careful of the fourth dimension.*'"

I asked, "What's the fourth dimension?"

"Orgasms."

During moments like these, I knew there was much to be learned in this whole track-down-elder-wisdom thing; after all, for years I've been laboring under the delusion that orgasms were a *good* thing.

———

THERE WAS ONE DEMOGRAPHIC SECTOR of my acquaintance who, when told that I was in search of the wisdom of older folks, sometimes became irritable or confused. These were men in their fifties. "Is that meant to be funny?" one of these gents asked me, with a slightly sour expression; another said, "I didn't know you were so interested in sciatica."

An eleven-year-old whom I'm friends with also expressed her reservations about my targeted demographic. "They may not have much to say," she counseled before glibly adding, "But good luck with that!"

Burro-like, I trudged onward.

{ 4. }

I hit the library. Given that I didn't have a strong idea of what wisdom is, I figured it behooved me to see what other people thought it was.

I quickly determined that the world is not lacking in theories on this front.

Muhammad Ali wrote, "Wisdom is knowing when you can't be wise."

Samuel Taylor Coleridge wrote, "Common sense in an uncommon degree is what the world calls wisdom."

Walter Benjamin wrote, "Counsel woven into the fabric of real life is wisdom."

Ecclesiastes tells us, "To fear the lord is the beginning of wisdom."

Theodore Roosevelt wrote, "Nine-tenths of wisdom consists of being wise in time."

Albert Einstein wrote, "A clever person solves a problem. A wise person avoids it."

Seneca wrote, "There is nothing the wise man does reluctantly. He escapes necessity because he wills what necessity is going to force on him."

Krishna says in the Bhagavad Gita, "The awakened sages call

a person wise when all his undertakings are free from anxiety about results."

William Blake wrote, "The road of excess leads to the palace of wisdom."

Patience Worth wrote, "A pot of wisdom would boil to nothing ere a doubter deemeth it worth tasting."

Nicolás Gómez Dávila wrote, "The stupidity of an old man imagines itself to be wisdom; that of an adult, experience; that of a youth, genius."

Benjamin Franklin wrote, "He's a fool that cannot conceal his wisdom."

Buddha wrote, "The fool who knows he is a fool is that much wiser."

Theories specific to the wisdom of older people were less abundant. The East's veneration of elders is rooted in history and tradition: in Taoism, attaining longevity has been seen as a sign of sainthood; Brahmanic canons record that a few elderly hermits became so wise that their bodies were transubstantiated into immortality. Confucianism promotes ancestor worship, which is certainly related to reverence for the elderly—just for the *deceased* elderly, thus making the reverence much easier to sustain.

My initial research suggested that the wisdom of elders is particularly venerated in Eastern and African cultures. And Middle Eastern. And Latin. And Native American and Australian Aboriginal. In other words, in all the cultures but the one I happened to be in.

In general, the more technological a culture, the less the wisdom of elders is valued; in a world in which megabytes and artificial intelligence are the coin of the realm, skills like passing on traditions and providing cultural context are perceived to have diminished worth.

If you want to be a sage, surround yourself with sagebrush.

———

I ALSO TRIED to read as many interviews with older people as possible. *80,* a book of interviews with eighty of the country's most famous eighty-year-olds, had just been published, so I bought it and read it.

To read eighty interviews given by primarily affluent white Americans is to have the prescription "Do something that you love" beaten into your head until you're ready to maim a small animal; indeed, this sentiment, along with "Stay involved," "Have a sense of humor," and "The young have no interest in history" are this book's breakfast, lunch, and dinner.

A few people in *80* individuated themselves, however. Don Hewitt said, "Was I devastated when they replaced me as executive producer of *60 Minutes*? I was, until a friend told me to think of *60 Minutes* as Yankee Stadium, the place that, even though Babe Ruth hadn't swung a bat there in more than half a century, is still known as 'The House That Ruth Built.' That did it. Devastation all gone."

Studs Terkel waxed plaintive: "Einstein never dreamed of Hiroshima when he approached Roosevelt and convinced him to build the atom bomb. When Einstein heard it was dropped on humans, he pulled out his hair and said, 'I don't know what the weapons of World War III will be. But I know the weapons of World War IV—sticks and stones.'"

Hollywood Squares host Peter Marshall encouraged young people not to take themselves too seriously—"as famous as you become, they won't know who the hell you are in thirty years. Ask a youngster about Bing Crosby or Al Jolson or Maurice Chevalier. They won't know. The guy who helped me and was my idol was Dick Haymes. Nobody remembers Dick Haymes."

Betty Garrett, who played the taxi driver in *On the Town*, said, "I never think of myself as old. I think my mirror is wrinkled."

Novelist and former Beat Herbert Gold said, "I have one

bit of advice for young people. Don't play golf. I mean it. It's boring."

Two THINGS I READ during this early period made a particularly strong impression on me. The first was the story that a seventy-nine-year-old Shirley Chisholm told to the authors of *A Wealth of Wisdom: Legendary African American Elders Speak* in 2004. Talking about her experience as the first black woman elected to Congress, Chisholm mentioned a congressman who sat in an aisle seat on the House floor.

Each day, when Chisholm showed up for work, the gentleman—who sat in front of her—would start coughing as soon as he saw her. Chisholm, concerned about his health, asked a colleague if the congressman was tubercular, and the colleague delivered some startling information. It seemed that, as soon as Chisholm walked by the coughing congressman each day, the congressman had developed a habit of pulling out a handkerchief and then spitting in it, as if spitting in Chisholm's face.

So Chisholm, fired up, decided to teach the man a lesson. She showed up at the House of Representatives the next day wearing a sweater with big pockets, in one of which she'd placed a man's handkerchief. The congressman started coughing, and Chisholm said to herself, Uh-huh, baby, I'm going to fix you today. At the moment that he pulled out his handkerchief, Chisholm pulled out her own. Then she spit in it and threw it in the man's face. "Beat you to it today," she told him.

Chisholm's fiery act did not go unnoticed by the onlookers and members of the press seated in the House's balcony—they started yelling, "Shirley, give it to him, give it to him," forcing the Speaker to beg for order.

Years later, taking a broader view on life, Chisholm summed up, "Whatever I do, even today, I look only to God and my conscience for approval, not man. That's my motto. You go crazy if you look to man. Follow the dictates of your conscience." ✓

———

EQUALLY ARRESTING TO ME was an essay that Martin Marty wrote in a book called *The Life of Meaning,* in which he espouses the theory that napping is a form of prayer. I called Marty one day, reaching him in his office in Chicago.

It's been said that if mainline Protestants could have elected a pope over the last few decades or so, that person would almost certainly have been Marty. A professor of religious history at the University of Chicago for thirty-five years, this Lutheran pastor is the author of more than fifty books, including the National Book Award–winning *Righteous Empire* and *Cry of Absence,* a reflection on the Psalms that he wrote after his first wife's death.

"So if napping is a form of prayer," I said to him, "then I guess I have to ask you how you define prayer."

"It's a constant, sustained, not-often-spoken communication with God, or the transcendent, or whatever you call it," the seventy-nine-year-old responded in excitable, boyish tones.

He elaborated: "When I ask people why they can't fall asleep when they want to nap, it always comes down to one of two things. (1) 'I didn't finish what I was going to do,' or (2) 'I have so much to do when I get up.' One is guilt and the other is worry. The act of prayer is an abandonment of both."

I asked, "So am I also praying when I'm unconscious or dead?"

"Yes. Emphatically."

I told him I thought it was a fascinating idea. I said, "My only worry is that all my prayers will be answered, but I won't know it because I'll be asleep."

"You'll know it when you wake up in the morning."

I remembered looking at Marty's Web site. A page called

"Hosting Martin Marty?" has various sections ("Receptions: Marty enjoys mixing with others at receptions," "Length of lecture: Unless otherwise specified, Marty speaks for exactly 50 minutes," "Meals: Marty prefers to breakfast alone"). The one called "Naps" stipulates, "After lunch and before an afternoon appearance or just before dinner, Marty typically takes a 7 to 10-minute refresher nap."

I asked him, "Did I read somewhere that when you nap you put your wristwatch on your forehead?"

"I used to. Now I time myself with my cellphone. I lay it down next to me."

"And that's simply to time yourself so that you won't take more than a fifteen- or twenty-minute nap?"

"No, no—not fifteen, that's way too long! I do seven to ten. If I fall into a deep sleep, then I get a knot in my stomach and I'm mopey. I started out at eighteen, then I was fifteen, then I was ten, now I'm eight."

"So you've been in prayer *training*."

"If the monks worked as hard at being monks as I do sleeping, we'd have a holy world."

{ 5. }

It occurred to me, early in my search, to interview the two older people whom I've spent the most amount of time with in my life, my mother and Will, my stepfather. The word "wise" would seem a likely designation in the case of my stepfather—one of the country's few authorities on coal gasification, this now-retired engineer is a history buff who likes to look at the big picture.

But my mother, a former social worker, comes to the designation in a somewhat more roundabout fashion. This is, after all, a woman who has on more than one occasion professed that electricity is created by tiny men who live inside our walls; a woman who, during a brief flirtation with Transcendental Meditation in the 1970s, was told to pick a euphonious, pleasure-inducing word for her mantra and so chose the woman's name Lenore. In 1996, when the topic of gay marriage was much in the news, Mom helped me with a journalistic stunt in which she and I showed up at various Manhattan hotels and restaurants claiming that I was about to marry my boyfriend in an elaborate ceremony. On Day 1, just outside the Waldorf-Astoria, I explained to Mom what I was going to tell the hotel's wedding planner—that I wanted to throw a sumptuous party for two hundred, at the reception of which Cirque de Soleil was to perform on the table-tops. Mom was unclear what Cirque de Soleil was—again, this was 1996—so I explained that it was a "Canadian circus troupe that performs without animals."

"With 'out' animals?" Mom asked.

"With no animals."

"Oh! I thought you meant gay animals. That sounded *very* interesting."

One *loves* Ann, but one wonders.

And yet something about her comment on the beach about having developed a "thick shell" around her feelings for Will made me think she had been doing some soul mining.

———

I RENTED A CAR and drove the five hours from New York up to where Mom and Will live. Although being at the wheel usually gives this city dweller a feeling of freedom and expansiveness, I was experiencing a certain amount of dread. It's always fraught to interview family members—what if you end up not including them in the finished story? This is compounded when the topic at hand is wisdom; not to include Mom and Will's statements would be to suggest that I didn't think them wise. I'd made sure to emphasize to them that I would be interviewing lots of people, so as to prepare them for possibly being superseded by greater luminaries.

And so, on a balmy Wednesday morning at about eleven, my mother and I settled into adjoining chairs in her and Will's sunny lakeside living room. Mom's patrician good looks were nicely set off by her mild restlessness and a lot of comfortable-looking black clothing: Barbara Bush at a yoga class. After she'd nimbly answered a couple of my questions, she looked at me and said, "Does it bother you that I'm knitting during this?"

"No."

Her knitting needles clicked and clacked like a tiny sword fight.

Mom said that she did indeed feel that she'd gotten wiser as she'd gotten into her seventies: "I have more stuff stored in my brain to make conclusions with. But I also have more scar tissue. ✓ You get more leery as you get older. I've slowed down." She went on to say, "We've misinterpreted Darwin. It's not survival of the fittest. It's survival of the most adaptable."

Then Mom and Will switched places—Will had been sitting in the kitchen. Will is striking to look at. Rail thin and possessed of a lugubrious voice and bulging, deep eyes, one of them glass, he looks like a character actor from a movie filmed in the shadier parts of a Moravian castle. Hear the plaintive howl of the werewolf.

While Mom had been all ease and self-deprecation during her interview, Will brought a sense of drama to his. Once seated, he said, "Wait just a minute before we begin"—he wanted to finish his cigarette, but it seemed as if he was trying to summon up something from within.

Then, his eyes starting to well, he said he was ready to begin. He then asked me not to repeat what he was about to tell me.

"But I'm going to write about it," I said, somewhat confused.

"That's different. That's fine. But don't talk about it. I don't want to be the subject of gossip."

I'm a little scared here.

Will proceeded to tell me that he's lost his confidence. His first wife died recently, and it had shaken him up. They'd been married twenty years when "disaster struck in the form of booze. I followed my prick, as guys do. I made some very bad decisions in my thirties and hurt a lot of people." When his daughter Martha called him to tell him about her mother, "It was as if I had been kicked in the gut by an animal. I broke down crying. Ever since then, I've felt that iron fucking door is clanging shut."

"But you've been thinking this way for a while, no?" I asked.

Two years earlier, Will had mailed my brother and two sisters and I a strange missive. A three-by-five note card bore the words, "Henry: In answer to a number (small) of enquiries over the years, I have decided to consign my wishes, in WRITING, to paper, for the days of planting time. Love, Will." An attached set of instructions detailed his wishes regarding hospitalization ("No extraordinary measures," "No major transplants such as liver, heart, penis, belly-button or small amount of brain left") and funeral ("Music (optional): Dave Brubeck's "Sweet William," Funeral at RC Church if they'll have me. I will check. If more convenient, get a Lithuanian priest from St. Casimers on Providence Street in Worcester"). He requested a "Simple stone: William P. Earley 1928–200? With a small inscription: 'He made a difference.' A small addition if no problem around the edge: a fly rod with line and fly."

Staring across the living room at the sparkly lake, Will explained that he'd been motivated to send us the letter after two ministrokes set off a depression. "I feel far less confident. Since those two strokes, every time I start walking, I count my steps. When I first started walking as a kid, I counted my steps." He continued, "Don't tell your mother this, but while she was away on her last trip, I got a doctor to give me Adderall, which is what they give ADD kids."

I wasn't sure where the wisdom was in this, so I steered the conversation back onto that topic.

Will invoked the serenity prayer used by Alcoholics Anonymous. Although he has fallen off the wagon a few times in the past forty or so years, Will has been a steadfast member of AA.

"It's 'wisdom to know the difference,' not '*the* wisdom to know the difference," he said. The AA version of the prayer, by Reinhold Niebuhr, runs, "God grant us the serenity to accept the things we cannot change; courage to change the things we can, and wisdom to know the difference."

Will added, "There's a fine line between the wisdom and wisdom. *The* wisdom is something you can put your hands on, something tangible. Wisdom is more evanescent. More intuitive than logical." He continued: "The goals we set for ourselves may give us direction, but they may also disappoint. I've achieved a lot in life, but it hasn't necessarily made me happy." He took a nine-months-pregnant pause here before saying, "I'm satisfied. But if it all stops tomorrow—so what?"

Now I was truly scared; even my *watch* stopped ticking. I asked, "You're not saying that you're going to . . . ?"

"No, I wouldn't do that. I wouldn't pull a trigger on my 'gats.'"

I sighed with relief. I added, "You've had a good life."

"I'm satisfied with my relationship with my kids. My first wife never bad-mouthed me to my kids, and that really helped. But I'm closer to you kids than I am to my own kids." He said he'd never talked about "any of this stuff" with his own kids, even though his son and one of his daughters lives in Massachusetts. "It wouldn't be hard to see them on a regular basis. But I don't want to see them on a regular basis."

"Why not?"

"I want them to have their own lives. I want them to make their own lives. Maybe it's because I've been so wrong in the past." He went on to say that he'd once given his son bad advice about the son's marriage, and that Will hadn't quite recovered from doing so.

We talked for an hour and a half. Will was exhausted by it. The three of us had been planning to go out for dinner—Mom was especially excited about this, because it was only the second time in a year that Will had wanted to.

But shortly after Will and I had finished talking, he said he was too tired, and so we decided to order in Chinese instead. Immediately after dinner, Will headed for his bedroom. Ah yes, I mused, thinking of my conversation with Martin Marty, maybe Will is praying.

I drove back to New York the next morning. That night, Will, who'd spent most of the day lying in bed, walked into the kitchen and told my mother, "I'm so exhausted from talking to Henry." Then he started talking in a kind of incoherent gibberish and proceeded to fall on the floor six times. Mom frantically put his boots on him, draped his parka over him, and poured him into the car. She rushed him to the emergency room, where she told the staff that she thought Will was stroking. But it gradually became clear that this was not the case; Will had taken a lot of Ambien. Mom's panic and concern quickly morphed into anger. Will had had a turn with Oxycontin some years before, at which point she had thrown him out of the house, letting him back only once he'd gone through a treatment program.

Then, three nights later, Will had to be taken back to the emergency room, this time by ambulance.

Shortly after he returned from the hospital, Mom found Will asking a neighbor for sleeping pills, so she asked Will to leave the house. Two days later, she asked for a divorce.

{ 6. }

When you're looking to learn, sometimes the best teacher is—and I hope you're sitting down for this—an actual teacher.

Not only has Harold Bloom taught literature at Yale for fifty-three consecutive years, but he is the author of a study of wisdom literature called *Where Shall Wisdom Be Found?* published in 2004. Traditionally, wisdom literature is those written works that poetically praise God and offer lessons about virtue—think the Book of Job or Ecclesiastes. But Bloom, as befits his reputation as an iconoclast—you may remember the controversy he stirred up in 1994 when his book *The Western Canon* attacked those who think reading has a social purpose rather than a purely aesthetic or reflective one and who thus think it important to get underrepresented minority writers onto college syllabi—asserts that works by writers such as Shakespeare and Cervantes and Emerson also qualify for the genre.

Would Bloom want to talk to someone whose approach to the topic of wisdom is nonacademic? I wasn't sure. His writing is sometimes so erudite as to leave my head spinning—at one point in *Where Shall Wisdom Be Found?* he writes, "What Plato, and his Socrates, know about the uses of etymology, particularly for the meaning of names, is finally Homeric." Rich with digressions and arcana, Bloom's early work is even *more* daunting: it's said that when he reread his book *The Anxiety of Influence* a year after its publication in 1973, even *he* didn't know what he was talking about. But throughout the years, his books have showcased a kind of perspicacity that is hard to deny—he defended the Romantics at a time when their stock in intellectual circles was very low; *The Anxiety of Influence* suggested that the history of poetry is fueled by poets who misread and then try to outdo, or express their resentment toward, their own favorite poets; he asserts that Shakespeare invented the world as we know it. In the blinding light of his intellectual bonfire, I am, by turns, fascinated, confused, irritated, bewildered, and inspired. But I am never bored.

I FIRED OFF AN E-MAIL to Bloom's Yale address, assuming I'd meet with silence. So you can imagine my surprise when I returned home that evening and found that there were two messages on my answering machine. The first was a distinguished, slightly winded tenor saying, "This is Harold Bloom—B, L, O, O, M." He said he'd gotten my e-mail and wondered if I could come talk to him in New Haven in three weeks' time. Excitedly, I pushed the "3" button on my phone to save the message. The next message on the machine, it turned out, was a strangely familiar voice: "Oh, sir, this is Harold Bloom again. I'm not sure you're aware that a few years ago I wrote a book called *Where Shall Wisdom Be Found?* In any case, my dear, it would be a great help if you read that before we talk."

I called Bloom the next morning, and we made an appointment. He told me, "I was just considering how ironic it is—the irony does not fall on you, of course—that the two wisest characters in Shakespeare, Sir John Falstaff and King Lear, are each just short of eighty, which I am approaching. How old are you, Mr. Alford?"

"Forty-five. A youngster."

"And you're writing a whole book about wisdom?"

"I am."

"A dark topic. A very dark topic."

The next day, I sat down to start reading *Where Shall Wisdom Be Found?* Bloom states early on that the book arose out of a personal need and reflects a "quest for sagacity that might solace and clarify the traumas of aging, of recovery from grave illness, and of grief for the loss of beloved friends." (In 1965, Bloom fell into a deep, almost year-long depression; he has also suffered over the years from both ulcers and heart attacks.) But the book is less a work of self-help or advice than it is a scholarly and hypererudite appreciation of various works of classical literature that can be read in order to "repair our solitude."

In addition to his talent for capturing the interrelationships between various writers, Bloom has always had a knack for coming up with the most beguiling quotations imaginable—the epigraph for his book on Shakespeare is from Nietzsche, "That for which we find words is something already dead in our hearts. There is always a kind of contempt in the act of speaking"—and *Where Shall Wisdom Be Found?* finds him in solid form. There are strong thoughts from Emerson and William James and Dr. Johnson gracefully woven into Bloom's arguments. What comes through by the end of the book, though, is his consuming passion for the works at hand. Shortly after finishing the book, I bought tickets to see Ian McKellen play Lear, and I also bought a copy of the collected works of Montaigne. Bloom had gotten me fired up.

———

BLOOM AND HIS WIFE, Jeanne, live in a three-floor, shingled house on a leafy street just off the Yale campus. Metal cane in hand,

Bloom hobbled to the door to greet me and asked me to call him Harold. Seemingly every article that has ever been written about Bloom mentions that he looks like Zero Mostel. I am unable to break from the pack here—he looks exactly like Zero Mostel.

We seated ourselves at a long, book-covered table in the dining room. A nimbus of cowlicky white hair imparted a boyishness to the otherwise lugubrious aspect of his plump, downturned lips and sad, knowing eyes.

"Go to it, my dear," he said, motioning with his hand for me to begin.

"What did you mean when you said, 'A very dark topic'?" I asked disingenuously, given that I had just watched the question of wisdom implode my mother's once-stellar marriage into a white dwarf of resentments.

He referred to *Where Shall Wisdom Be Found?* and said, "I remember at one point quoting a wonderful remark of William Butler Yeats where he said, 'Man can incarnate the truth but he cannot know it.'" (This is in the last letter Yeats wrote.) "And I wrote that with wisdom it's just the opposite—you absolutely cannot incarnate wisdom, but you can at least know what it is."

"You also write that wisdom is 'a Perfection that can either absorb or destroy us.'"

"Which is why, on the whole, I would rather not absorb too much wisdom. I'll be seventy-seven in July." He looked down at his slightly shaky hands and, starting to smooth a stray piece of paper lying on the table, continued, "I also quoted Samuel Johnson—'Love is the wisdom of fools and the folly of the wise.' That's a very dark statement."

I allowed as how it was.

The closest Bloom comes to providing an out-and-out definition of wisdom in *Where Shall Wisdom Be Found?* is when he quotes the Talmudic text *Pirke Aboth,* or *Sayings of Our Fathers:* "Hillel used to say: If I am not for myself, who is for me? And when I am for myself what am I? And if not now, when?" Calling the passage "perfect, balanced wisdom," Bloom explains the quote thusly: "I affirm myself, but if I am for myself only, it is inadequate, and unless standing up both for myself and for others happens right now, whenever can it happen?"

———

HOPING TO ELICIT SOME PRACTICAL ADVICE, I brought up the fact that Bloom likes to read Jonathan Swift's *A Tale of a Tub* twice a year to "subdue" himself.

"Indeed," he replied, "I now know the book by heart and, as with a great many poems, I think that at this very moment I could give you the entire thing. There's a strange part of it that is absolutely insane—deliberately insane—called 'A Digression on Digressions.' Do you want some water?"

"No, thanks."

Looking down at his cane, he explained, "This is only momentary. I've pulled a muscle," and then shambled into the nearby kitchen. The meta quality of the moment was not lost on me: while talking about a digression on digression, Bloom had launched into his own digression.

He returned with a mug full of water and said, "What were you asking?"

I stared at the mug. It appeared to be embossed with a photograph of Bloom and his wife.

"Uh, so you read *A Tale of a Tub* twice a year, and you like to reread Plato's *Republic* to 'chasten' your 'fury against all ideology.'"

"Yes. Plato is the first person who rejects the aesthetic in favor of ideology. And in that sense he is the first representative of Platonists who have largely destroyed academic study in the United States. The School of Resentment types. Ideologues of one sort or another. The feministas, the sexual orientationists, the Marxistas, the so-called New Historicists who are just Foucault–and–soda water. The whole schlemozzle. They've totally destroyed the subject because why in hell would a student spend his or her time working through the intellectual intricacies of *Beloved* by Toni Morrison or *Meridian* by Alice Walker? Which are, of course, supermarket fiction . . . But *you* talk."

"Right. Well, I'm interested in this idea that as we age, we lose our memory but we gain something else."

"In my case, I haven't lost my memory."

My mind flashed onto an image of Bloom growing up in his family's Orthodox household in the Bronx. By age five, he'd taught himself to read Yiddish, Hebrew, and English; by ten, he'd memorized much of Hart Crane and William Blake. He's said that in his youth he could read one thousand pages an hour. One night as an undergraduate at Cornell, Bloom, drunk, recited Hart Crane's long poem "The Bridge" word by word, backward.

"OK," I said, not wanting to labor the point. "But what have you gained with age?"

He took a long pause before answering, "A healthier respect and affection for my wife than I used to have. And I don't think she can hear me saying that. She's in the kitchen." A sly smile crossed his face as he added, "Next May will be our fiftieth anniversary."

———

Bloom's tenderness took me by surprise. A friend had warned me that Bloom would call me "my dear" roughly thirty times during the course of an interview, but I would have thought that he'd be the last person to wax all sweetie-pie in the presence of a stranger.

In talking to him, the general impression I got was of a hardworking schoolteacher who is dedicated to the common reader.

"I could give up teaching—I could afford to," he told me at one point. "I could give up writing, I could afford to. I could give up my Chelsea House"—his series of books of essays about specific authors, each with an introduction by Bloom—"but I don't want to. I want to go on doing all three activities because I think I have always been a common reader myself."

But certainly all this output and dedication is aided greatly by the support and ministrations of a forbearing partner. Indeed, the Blooms' lovely interconnectedness was exhibited a few minutes later when the phone rang and Bloom answered it: a student calling to dispute a grade Bloom had given him.

"Hello?" Bloom said. "Yes, it is . . . Oh—no, no, no. The more I've reflected on our conversation the unhappier I've become. I do not wish to discuss this further. We have at Yale a vast collection of deans within deans within deans. If you feel any wrong or injustice has been done to you, I urge you to invoke a dean or two."

Click!

"That was infuriating!" Bloom harrumphed. He swiveled his body to direct his voice toward the kitchen. "Darling, if the phone rings again, will you answer? If it's him, tell him that your husband has just died."

————

BLOOM CALLS HIMSELF a heretical, Gnostic Jew. Gnosticism, which started in pre-Christian times and flourished until the fifth century, asserts that the universe is alienated from God as a result of a primal, blitzkrieg-like splitting. If Christianity and Judaism and almost all pagan beliefs hold that the soul reaches its proper end through faith and good works or grace or some much-debated alloy thereof, Gnosticism suggests that this destination is arrived at as a result of a quasi-intuitive knowledge of the mysteries of the universe that only a few enlightened individuals possess. Gnosticism rejects all worldly authorities out-side the self, and it proposes that we are divine souls trapped in a physical world by an evil spirit called the demiurge.

I wondered how all this bleakness and darkness of vision col-ored Bloom's idea of spiritual advancement and education, so I asked, "Do you think that the getting of wisdom usually neces-sitates pain or suffering?"

"No. Nietzsche thought so. But that's because he thought all memorability was based on pain. In a way he's right, but in another way he's wrong. But I must say, now that I'm getting old, sometimes I lie awake at night—I usually lie awake at night, I have trouble sleeping—and, dear Henry, I find myself increas-ingly realizing that when I yield to involuntary memory rather than try to force the memory to come, the things that I remem-ber? It's the embarrassing moments one remembers."

"So that would bear Nietzsche's theory out."

"Yes. But I've tried to apply it to other things. For years, my only test for a poem was, Is it so inevitable in its phrasing for me that I instantly memorized it on first reading? I thought that from a Nietzschean point of view then that was because it gave me pain rather than pleasure. I tried to work out that dialectic, since if poetry is not pleasure, then what is it?"

Bloom seems to answer the question himself in *Where Shall Wisdom Be Found?* when he writes that memorizing poems can help you to "think more comprehensively."

I asked him what exactly he meant by this.

"When you possess by memory . . . ," he started. "Well, think of what it means in general, Henry, to possess by memory. We lose people inevitably. And when we lose people, we lose them except for memory."

"So, are you saying that memory is a hedge against loss?"

"There are no hedges against loss. So rephrase it, my dear."

"So, memory is a . . . a . . . an aid for . . . What word would you use?"

"Memory plays an important part in the role of cognition. I don't think that you can think clearly, well, and accurately unless you can remember a great deal of the very strongest and most eloquent and wise matters that have been said and thought. I take it that that is what education is about."

———

TALKING TO BLOOM made me realize that I have very little grounding in wisdom literature. Or anything at all, if you must know.

So I hit the library again, this time holing up for a period of days. I was overwhelmed by the amount of stuff I found; this was dense reading, full of words like "Zoroastrianism" and "ontogeny." Worse, no one has yet published a comprehensive history of wisdom literature—there is no *Oxford Companion to Wisdom*, nor even a *WizLit for Dummies*.

The term "wisdom," as I had sensed earlier, has had roughly eight million definitions over the course of history. Every culture, according to Kurt Rudolph, a professor of the history of religion at Philipps-Universität in Marburg, Germany, has had its ideal of wisdom and has recorded it either orally or in writing. "If religion can broadly be conceived as a way of coping theoretically and practically with the problems of the world, nature, and society," Rudolph writes in *The Encyclopedia of Religion*, "then wisdom is one part of this effort."

To try to condense, or even explain, the history of wisdom into one neat little package seems insurmountable—indeed, Rudolph says it would be impossible. But you *can* say, as Rudolph does, that wisdom has taken three broad forms: "an anthropological ability to cope with life (the oldest and most widespread form); a rational system (interpretation of the cosmos, philosophy, beginnings of science); and a personification, hypostasis, goddess, or attribute of God."

Over the course of history, wisdom has been both a part of and an antagonist to religion in the Western world. In its latter role, it was a secular and profane way of dealing with the hassles and obstacles of life that fell outside the gates of specific gods or priests or cults and thus paved the way for scientific thinking. (Chinese wisdom, by contrast, has minimal connections to religion; among the cardinal virtues that typify the Confucian wise man are a command of language; knowledge of human nature and society; and adherence to Confucian rules more akin to conduct guides.) As with its form, the tone of wisdom is variable, too—it can be sticky sweet or witheringly dark, a Tuesday with Morrie or a breakfast in hell.

WHEN I TELL YOU what the prescriptions and helpful suggestions offered by some of the earliest wisdom literature were, you will think I am making them up. Come with me now to what is currently called Iraq, but imagine that it is five thousand years ago. This is Sumer, the earliest known civilization. Follow me along the banks of the Euphrates, being careful not to trip on the irrigation ditches and canals; dodge the slow-moving cart made possible by the recent invention of the wheel; and duck with me into a small building constructed out of reeds. Here we find what we're looking for: clay tablets on which the Sumerians have preserved their practical advice for daily living. And what do the staggeringly profound writings on these tablets say? Let's look at two examples: "He who possesses much silver may be happy" and "We are doomed to die, let us spend."

And you wondered why you aren't planning your next vacation to Sumer.

Starting with works like the fragmentary *Counsels of Shurup-*

pak (a Babylonian book of proverbs from ca. 2500 B.C.) and *The Precepts of Ptah-Hotep* (the oldest surviving Egyptian work of wisdom, dating to 2200 B.C. and containing the directive "Be not puffed up with thy knowledge, and be not proud because thou are wise"), we get the idea that a wise person is a member of a community who is self-controlled and whose wisdom is partly defined by his skill at crafts and arts. The Akkadian word for a teacher of wisdom, *"ummanu,"* is derived from the Sumerian term for "master craftsman."

Prior to Socrates, wisdom was not usually a topic itself; it is assumed. But over time, from preclassical to classical to Christian eras, wisdom shifts, Rudolph writes, from subject to object, and "an anthropological capacity for insight becomes a form of revelation about the cosmos or God. The content of wisdom as insight into the coherence of the world and life takes on a religious and, to some extent, esoteric character (as in the Wisdom of Solomon, Gnosticism, and Mahayana Buddhism)."

First it's a seed. Then it's a tree that needs sunlight.

THOUGH IT'S SOMEWHAT REDUCTIONIST to do so, I like to think that, over the course of time, either directly or by example, each great thinker and teacher highlights a major component of wisdom.

Confucius (551 B.C.–479 B.C.) stressed the importance of reciprocity. Once, when asked if there was a principle by which you should live your life, he said, "Is not reciprocity such a word? What you do not want done to yourself, do not do unto others."

Buddha (ca. 563 B.C.–483 B.C.) made the valuable contribution of nonattachment. He emphasized that we suffer when we fixate on our thoughts; the first line of the *Dhammapada,* a collection of his wise sayings, is, "We are what we think."

Socrates (470 B.C.–399 B.C.) brought doubt to the party. He was the first person to systematically inquire into the nature of wisdom; intriguingly, however, he did not think himself wise. But when a friend of his asked the oracle at Delphi if there was any man in Athens wiser than Socrates, the oracle said no. This prompted Socrates' quest: he approached various Athenian men who were considered wise—poets, artisans, statesmen—and, after talking to them, gauged that they were, in fact, not. So Socrates concluded that the oracle was correct: while most men thought they were wise but were not, Socrates *knew* he was not wise, and thus, paradoxically, was.

———

RECIPROCITY. Nonattachment. Doubt. Leaving the library one day, I started to think, These are such Big Questions, it's no wonder that philosophers and thinkers have been batting them about for thousands of years. But who has the time to ponder these questions these days? Who has his eye on the big picture and is ready to lead us into the future? Rushing to an appointment, I got in a cab, the driver of which proceeded to monologize for fifteen minutes about matters ranging from the geopolitical scene to reality television to the inhumanity of bike messengers who don't heed traffic signals. I thought, Too bad the people with all the answers today are busy driving cabs.

———

AFTER RECEIVING IMPORTANT INPUT over the years from the likes of Saint Augustine, Saint Thomas Aquinas, Montaigne, Francis Bacon, Descartes, and Locke, wisdom literature flourishes today, as evidenced by the near inescapability, at weddings or on yearbook pages, of selections from Khalil Gibran's *The Prophet*.

In our age of confession and celebrity, the two chief venues for celebrating life lessons are the memoir and the magazine profile or interview. In the former genre, the category leaders are the recollections of living during the Holocaust penned by

Anne Frank (*The Diary of a Young Girl*) and Elie Wiesel (*Night*). The latter takes its most fully realized form in *Esquire* magazine's monthly feature "What I've Learned," in which notable people unpack their troubled minds, as Ray Charles, then blind for sixty-seven years, did in 2003 with the gem "It would be a real bitch if I ever lost my hearing. I know I couldn't be no Helen Keller. That would be worse than death."

A hybrid of these two contemporary genres can be found, in the form of quotations, on the sides of Celestial Seasonings teas and cardboard coffee cups. The connection between wisdom and warm beverages is mysterious and perhaps best left to a scholar with a stronger interest in diuresis.

————

TWO THINGS STRUCK ME about this leg of my wisdom research. The first was that shorter is always better. As I pored over texts, I found that the ones that I was drawn to, and continued to think about after I had closed them, were those that contained miniversions of their philosophies, like "We are what we think." It's no mistake that the first landmark work of wisdom literature—the *I Ching,* or *Book of Changes*—is a collection of aphorisms, nor that it inspired other important collections of aphorisms such as the *Tao-te Ching* and Confucius's *The Analects*. (Confucius once said that if he had fifty years to devote himself to the *I Ching,* then he might finally know something.) Yes, an interest in succinctness bespeaks a short attention span. But there's nothing more powerful than the artful distillation of an entire philosophy down into a few words. Brevity kills.

————

THE SECOND THING that I took away from my research was the universality of wisdom. Take, for instance, Confucius's aforementioned "What you do not want done to yourself, do not do unto others." Doesn't it remind you of something once said by a certain long-haired from Galilee?

Or look at the topic of nonattachment. It's possible to draw a line from Buddha's "We are what we think" to Krishna's statement that a person is wise "when all his undertakings are free from anxiety about results" to nineteenth-century German philosopher Arthur Schopenhauer's belief that happiness "consists in extinguishing the will" to twentieth-century fashion doyenne Diana Vreeland's pronouncement "Elegance is refusal."

Or look at the virtue of doing with less. Belief in it seems to have traveled from ancient Greece (Epicurus: "A man is wealthy in proportion to the things he can do without") to nineteenth-century Germany (Nietzsche: "Whoever possesses little is possessed by that much less") to nineteenth-century New England (Thoreau: "A man is rich in proportion to the things he can do without") to contemporary Dublin (musician Sinead O'Connor: "I do not want what I haven't got").

Harold Bloom once famously said, "There are no poems, only relations between poems." What I think—emphasis on *think*—Bloom was driving at here is something similar to his theory of poetic influence. This theory suggests that poets respond to their precursors through misreading or "willful revisionism"—that is, they write slightly different versions of poems that have already been written by other poets. So what Bloom is really saying is "There is only one poem." But that doesn't have quite the heft or spank of "There are no poems," does it?

Bloom's "no poems" quote always struck me as slightly crazy-assed, until one day when I was looking for a recipe for sugar cookies. Consulting five different and far-ranging sources, including one from the 1800s, I found five virtually identical recipes. This reminded me of the time that I was reading a seventeenth-century Restoration comedy and came across the line "Pretentious? Moi?"—a bit of shtick that has rung, or tried to, through the ages. The past, as they say, is but prologue to the future.

So there are no sugar-cookie recipes, there are only relations between sugar-cookie recipes. There are no jokes, there are only relations between jokes. And maybe there is no wisdom, there are only relations between bits of wisdom.

What intrigues me about the overlap in wise sayings is that you could find a lot of differences between Confucius's and Jesus's religions—or between either of the other two groups of people—but their wisdom is pretty similar. So maybe wisdom, in tending to deal in abstractions, is more universal than religion. ✓

As someone who looks out into the world and sees religious fundamentalism as the cause of so many of the world's ills—suicide bombers, anyone? intolerance, anyone?—this gives me hope.

I find that this universality draws me into the church called wisdom. I don't like groups, so I'm a little squirrelly about entering.

But I am also excited.

Most of my communications with my mother, in the weeks directly after she'd asked Will for a divorce, were by e-mail. E-mail has been a boon to our family: my mom was able to keep all four of us kids and my sister-in-law, Jocelyn, up to date on her emotional state. Which was, as to be expected, ragged.

One of Mom's e-mails recounted some of her trauma and then said, "But you know all about this," an allusion to my 2000 breakup from a ten-year-long relationship, the details of which I've never spelled out for my mother, as it might necessitate a discussion of my genitals and their predilections. But I tried to be as available as possible to Mom in her time of need and to convey to her my sorrow and sympathy. At the same time, though, I didn't want to be a source of obligation to her, someone who needed answering. This was a complicated balance to strike.

That my mother was seventy-nine at this traumatic point in her life filled me with two opposing emotions. On the one hand, it seemed especially poignant to sever yourself from a companion at a time when you most want one for both practical and spiritual reasons. But on the other hand, her age made me worry less about her ability to emotionally right herself, because she'd had to do it so many times before. When I ended my ten-year relationship, it took me a year to be wholly myself again. Ultimately, my salvation lay in frequent and prolonged bouts of swimming—I left my "divorce," I once told a friend, on the bottom of the NYU pool—but it took me six or seven months to figure out that I had to swim my pain away. The next time I'm dealt an equally painful experience, I'll know right away to buy a new bathing suit.

I knew that Mom also deals with emotional trauma through activity, and on this front I knew she was well equipped: she's a crossword-puzzle fiend and a player of word games, a gardener, a knitter, a watercolorist, a yoga dabbler, and a bridge player. Stasis is not an option.

People sometimes ask me if I feel in any way responsible for my mother's divorce. I don't. Possibly I feel a small amount of responsibility vis-à-vis its timing—Will's interview had had some of the flavor of a deathbed confession. But, obviously, the divorce would have happened with or without me. I was merely yeast.

———

EVERY APRIL, five or six members of my family go to my sister Kendy's house in Durham, North Carolina, and attend a documentary film festival called Full Frame. Over the course of a long weekend, we get dispatches from the hellholes and eccentric byways of the globe, we wax emotional, we laugh, and we eat a lot of barbecue. The ringleader here is Kendy—at fifty-eight, the oldest of us kids and easily the most loved person in the family. Tomboyish and great fun and a little kooky, Kendy is our Kathy Bates in Birkenstocks. She recently knit a pair of size 23 socks that she's hoping to get to Shaquille O'Neal. She and her husband, Rick, a paleontologist, once spent a year trekking the Incan Highway one thousand miles through the Andes; they adopted two amazing kids, and they like to go on months-long bike trips that start in Europe and end in Asia.

This year, for the first time in our six years of going to the festival, Mom had come without Will; after she'd kicked him out, he'd gone to his son's house and from there to a crisis-treatment center in New Bedford. On the first night of Full Frame, Will had called and left a message on Kendy's machine. Mom had been avoiding his calls, and he wanted her to turn on her cellphone so he could talk with her.

The next day, as Mom and I were handing in our audience ballots for a troubling but wonderful movie about Uganda ("I was going to give it a nine out of ten," Mom told me confidentially, "but I don't know where Uganda is"), I noticed something.

"I see you haven't turned your cellphone on," I said.

"Fifty ways to leave your lover," she replied.

———

THAT EVENING, after dinner, as our group of six sat on the brick patio behind Kendy and Rick's house, Kendy told Mom, "Will called again and said to turn your phone on. Tone of voice: slightly pleading."

"I'm saying no to him," Mom said. "He told me that when I came down here that you guys would only cement my feelings."

"And have we?" Kendy asked.

"No."

"You'd mixed that sand and water long before you'd left," Kendy diagnosed.

"Exactly. I don't need you-all for that," Mom said. "All I need from you guys is full and total approval every five minutes."

———

PRIOR TO THE FESTIVAL, Kendy and Mom and I had decided to peel off from the moviegoing one afternoon to look at possible retirement communities—or, as Mom calls them, "finishing schools"—for her in Durham. Three years earlier, Mom had expressed a vague yearning for her (and Will) to move close to Kendy because "she'd push my wheelchair." At the time, I'd asked, "Do you really want to move away from all your friends in Massachusetts?" and she'd told me, "If you can make friends easily in Massachusetts, you can make friends easily in Durham."

Mom and Kendy and I had looked at retirement communities in Durham once before. We'd had a strange visit during that go-round on which we'd been given a tour by one of the facility's residents rather than by an employee. Somehow, this old bat got it into her mind that the best possible tour would start with a fifteen-minute overview of the artwork in the lobby, followed immediately by a brisk plunge into the residence's medical ward. There, we stumbled onto a scene that has been permanently imprinted on my brain: five limp, totally beleaguered residents—all women—were seated around a television set whose screen was pure snow; one of the women was clutching a doll whose single eye was a clothes button.

Our tour guide whispered to us, "Oh, they're watching the hockey game."

Mom and Kendy and I shared a communal silent scream of horror.

At the end of the tour, our guide's final gloss on the community was "We're a little unique because we're both independent living *and* assisted living. So you start out in independent living and then you sliiiiiiiiiiiiiiiiiide."

Mom and Kendy and I spent the next year making references to "the hockey game" and to sliiiiiiiiiiiiiding.

THIS TIME AROUND the retirement-community wheel, we found two strong contenders. At the first, an ebullient marketing director introduced us to various residents and employees. "This is

Becky," she said to Mom at one point. "She's the one who will keep you in shape."

"Many have tried," Mom said.

Strangely, I'm virtually unable to walk into a retirement home without thinking of those shots in science-fiction movies where slo-mo spacecraft glide and float across a backdrop of galaxies to one of the more popular Strauss waltzes. As soon as I see my first scooter in the lobby or my first tufty white-haired nonagenarian waft by at 1.2 miles per hour, I find myself slowing down and moving my arms in a way that I can describe only as floaty. My speech slows down, too, to a drawn-out "Hallooooo . . ." Indeed, when I met Becky, my hand waving hello described exactly the arc of a car's windshield wiper in first gear.

We zipped by the health center—"The care here is phenomenal," our guide informed us. "You will not smell *anything*." But we could definitely smell the pool, which had been chlorinated by a very heavy hand; Mom opined, "Oooh, that'd melt the suit right off you."

Our guide showed us a mimeographed copy of the activities schedule. I pointed out to Mom and Kendy that one of the activities was called "Reminiscin'." Kendy mimed looking out at an imaginary group of seniors and yelled out, "Who can remember what they had for breakfast?"

———

WHEN WE LOOKED at one of the model apartments, Mom became palpably excited and said, "This is the size I'm thinking and the apartment I'm thinking of. This is it."

Kendy urged, "Lie down on the floor and refuse to move!"

But Mom liked the second place—a community called Croasdaile—even more. After our tour, she said, "I think I'll go home and put the house on the market."

Kendy started singing, "I'm gonna wash that man right outta my hair . . ."

AT THE END of the film festival, the six of us were sitting around Kendy and Rick's dining-room table. Through an emissary—my sister JP, who has always been Will's closet link among the kids—Mom had sent a message to Will that she'd be willing to talk with him the following night.

Kendy asked Mom, "What are you going to say to Will?"

Without a beat, Mom said, "I've made my plans for the rest of my life, and they don't include you."

There was a collective intake of breath from all of us. The directness was bracing.

Kendy broke the silence. "You want to role-play that a little?"

"OK," Mom agreed.

Kendy started in as Will. "Ann, I love you. I'm trying to get better."

"I realize you are. But this problem has been going on for a while, and I gave you your chances."

"I want to live in West Brookfield. That's my home."

Mom said, "You can certainly live in West Brookfield, but I don't think either of us could swing the house by ourselves financially. But you could certainly get an apartment for yourself."

"But I want to live with you in the house, Ann."

"No, that won't work out. I've made different plans."

This interaction was incredibly difficult to watch, and I found myself almost unable to speak. I kept looking at my boyfriend and my sister's husband and my brother's wife—all of the people who'd linked their lives to Alfords—and wondering if they weren't mentally putting themselves in Will's position, perhaps getting a taste of what the consequences of a fall from grace might be.

Once Kendy had dropped her Will character, she said, "Boy, you are tough, Mom!"

"I am. I'm a tough old bird. I have to be. I'd like to be feminine and accommodating, but I can't."

———

THE NEXT DAY, a big storm shut down the Raleigh-Durham airport, and our flights were canceled. So five of us decided to rent a car and drive north. After about ten hours of arduous driving—not only was it raining part of the way, but we drove through Virginia listening to the Virginia Tech shootings story unfold on NPR—we pulled into New York City at about midnight. Mom and my sister-in-law Jocelyn—who'd done a lot of the driving—refused my invitation to spend the night at Greg's and my apartment. Jocelyn got back behind the wheel and, at 1:30 a.m., she and Mom got into Hartford, where Jocelyn lives and where Mom had left her car.

Jocelyn pleaded with Mom to spend the night and do the seventy-five-minute drive to her own house in the morning.

But Mom wouldn't. She got into her car and kept driving.

{ 8. }

The decisions we make can yield more pain than we expect.

I'd asked sociologist Setsuko Nishi to lunch. The eighty-six-year-old Nishi is famed for her devotion to both academia (she is professor emerita of sociology at Brooklyn College and the Graduate School of the City University of New York) and to community outreach. Currently she is the chief investigator on a national study of the long-term effects of wartime incarceration on Japanese Americans.

We were seated in the middle of a brightly lit, midtown Manhattan restaurant, and Nishi—tiny and patrician, turned out in a navy pantsuit and a string of pearls—was telling me something she started telling people only recently.

Like 120,000 other Japanese Americans, Nishi was put in an internment camp during World War II. Although she is quick to tell you that her experience was not a typical one, because she was in her camp only five months, she is less quick to tell you something else.

When Nishi was allowed to leave the Santa Anita Assembly Center at age eighteen to go to Washington University, she was told that if she was willing to work for her room and board, a second incarcerated Japanese-American student would also be sprung from the camp and sent to college. Nishi, of course, agreed. After saying good-bye to her parents and brother, who did not get out of the camp for another two years or so, she soon found herself babysitting and helping to prepare meals in the home of her host family, near Washington's campus in St. Louis.

"I made a secret vow that, with all this lovely food and shelter and a second family, I would never take a second helping of food while my parents and brother were still in the camp," Nishi told me. "But one night we were sitting around the dinner table, and the mother said to me, 'Suki, this is your favorite dish, won't you have some more?' I said no, thank you. She said, 'But this is your favorite. I know you like it.' I started crying, I just couldn't help it. I left the table. I said, 'I'm sorry I have to go.'"

Nishi's eyes misted up as she recounted the painful memory.

I asked, "How come you're able to talk about it now?"

"When I first said it, someone asked me that, too—'How come you chose here to say that?' There are things that you don't reveal. But I said that I thought it was important to show that there are a lot of feelings here. I want people to know that there's a lot of residue here. That everything is not all OK. That there are probably still things here that will probably never go away."

I nodded my head.

She added, "Some people say to me, 'How come you're not bitter?' and I'll say, 'Well, how do you know I'm not?'"

NISHI'S MAIN WORK has been on American race relations, focusing on institutionalized discrimination in complex social systems. She worked with famed African-American sociologist Horace Cayton in Chicago and wrote the pamphlet "Facts about Japanese Americans" (1946) before getting her doctorate in sociology from the University of Chicago. She served for three decades on the New York State Advisory Committee to the U.S. Commission on Civil Rights and was the founding president of the Asian American Federation of New York. After sixty years of work, she remains active.

I wouldn't like to try to distill Nishi's intellectual mandate down to a unifying operating principle or two. Fortunately, I don't need to, because she has done it for us. When Nishi won the 2007 Lifetime Achievement Award from the Association for Asian American Studies, she made a brief acceptance speech in which she asked the audience to "please indulge an old academic's reference to a couple of themes that thread through my work . . . One is that members of categorically discriminated-against groups are likely to find it more effective to use a socially supported mode of achievement, an alternative to what is pervasively promoted in Western society—that is, an individualistic, competitive mode. Another theme is the utility, for persons and for groups, of balance between, on the one hand, instrumental achievement and, on the other, expressive gratification—or, between what historically has been symbolized as masculine and feminine, or reason and emotion, or utility and esthetics, or—my favorite—beauty and function." Then, citing all of her own social supports by name— her parents and siblings; her late husband of fifty-seven years, artist Ken Nishi, and their five children; her mentors, colleagues, and students—she concluded, "Clearly, whatever of achievement there may be in my life and work has been via a socially supported achievement mode, not an individualistic competitive one and has proved to be an enormously gratifying and continuing pursuit of beauty and function." (Emphasis hers.)

———

IN THE RESTAURANT, I drew Nishi out on the idea of socially supported modes. She told me, "Frequently, the remedy that is suggested to groups who are discriminated against is a change in the individual. Individuals are encouraged to succeed. When they do succeed, they often lose contact with the people they leave behind. It can be very counterproductive when people assimilate. Those who succeed often feel alienated and unhappy." She added, "Today, with minorities, so much emphasis is put on self-help and self-improvement rather than dealing with the system."

I asked about the Japanese-American experience vis-à-vis socially supported modes. She said, "When the United States decided that it could no longer keep the Japanese Americans in internment camps, they urged them not to get together or form organizations. Roosevelt even thought it would be a good idea if we scattered all the Japanese—a couple per county all through the United States."

"I had no idea."

"The ones who succeeded were ruthless and brash. Some of us have that side in us. I surprise people sometimes. I'll be very polite, but maybe I'm the only minority around, and the chairman of a committee is ignoring me—"

"So you get right in there?" I guessed.

"Absolutely. I'll say, 'Mr. Chairman, I've been raising my hand for quite some time now.' Then he'll back off."

"Is this related to why your father used to call you 'my little Jack Dempsey'?" I asked, remembering Nishi's citation of her father in her acceptance speech.

"There was one Sunday afternoon. He took us to the park. My brother and I were playing in the sandbox, and some older kids came and took away my sand pail. So I went right over to them and"—here she stretched out her index and middle fingers and made a jabbing motion—"poked them in the eye. My father was very strict about me being ladylike," she said of the Los Angeles real-estate and insurance broker who, under the Alien Land Law, could not own property himself and so formed a family corporation of which six-year-old Setsuko was the secretary. "But he also wanted me to stand up for what is right."

———

A FEW MINUTES LATER, as she started to negotiate her fork around a delicately browned piece of cod that was seated on a small mound of sautéed spinach on her plate, Nishi looked at me and said, "I have benign hand tremors. So don't worry."

I didn't.

"Some people notice and don't mention it," she said. "So I do."

"That's a good policy," I offered. "My mother has difficulties hearing, so if she's at a meal where she doesn't know the people all that well, she'll turn to the person on either side of her and say, 'If any of my comments tonight seem absurdist, don't take it personally.'"

"That's very clever of her."

"It cuts her a lot of slack."

I asked Nishi if old age—or, rather, the emotional distance from the past that age brings—hasn't made it easier for people to talk about their experiences in the camps. She said that, yes, that was part of it but that there was something more. She said she was somewhat amazed by the amount of energy that former incarcerees put into trips back to the camps. "They don't want their memories to disappear," she said, alluding to the memorializing workshops and museum displays and theatrical productions that some of these people were engaged in. "The irony of course is that my generation tried very hard to forget about their experiences in the camps. But now they're gung-ho with supporting the memory. They were not able to do so individually. But in a collective way they're able to deal with it."

———

NISHI STILL OWNS THE DENIM DUFFEL BAG that her father told her to put her belongings into when their family went off to the camp. She takes it when she lectures at schools.

"I tell kids, 'If you had to leave your home and had to put everything that's important to you in this bag, what would you take?' That really shakes them up. That gets them thinking. It moves them in a way that they may not be able to verbalize, about what it would mean to be separated. To be ousted. Stigmatized."

"Most Americans don't realize that incarceration happened without a charge or a trial," I said, not mentioning that I myself was in this group forty-eight hours earlier, before I'd read my research materials for my interview with Nishi.

"We didn't do anything wrong. We didn't do anything illegal. Our parents didn't do anything illegal."

"It flies in the face of everything you're told about being an American," I said. "It says you are not protected under these laws."

"It's terribly disillusioning. Intellectually, the most disillusioning thing is that we believe in the Constitution. That's what really burns."

———

AFTER LUNCH, I walked Nishi down Fifth Avenue to an Asian American Federation board meeting that she had to attend. She is barely five feet tall, and in the streams of pedestrian traffic, I felt protective toward her. I found myself leaning my body in toward hers, as if our combined mass might prove a more effective shield against the oncoming hordes.

She told me that she has agreed to leave a collection of her files to UCLA. I started thinking about what sixty years' worth of research would look like—the sheer mass of it, the bulk. (Nine months later, I read in William F. Buckley's obituary that the papers the archconservative had bequeathed to Yale weighed seven tons.)

I soon found myself complimenting Nishi on her professional longevity. I said that many people would have been tempted to throw in the towel a long time ago.

Pulling herself slightly away so as to better direct her smile at me, she said, "But there's so much more to do."

Mom and Will decided that Will would buy her half of the house from her. This seemed like a win-win solution.

But then, about a week after the film festival, Mom sent us four kids an e-mail titled "Weird Plans." The weird plan was that Will was going to come back to the house, and he and Mom would live there together until Mom moved to Durham, which she imagined would be within a couple of months. Her plan was to move into an apartment during the typical one- or two-year wait to get into the finishing school.

This did not strike everyone as being the best possible move.

So when Mom happened to mention to me that one of her nearby senior centers was hosting a day trip to Mohegan Sun, the casino in southeastern Connecticut, it occurred to me that such a trip might provide a much-needed diversion.

———

IN RECENT YEARS, my mother's and my relationship has been based on adventure and escapism. It started in 1994 when Mom, hearing that my then-boyfriend Jess and I were going to Italy, nominated herself as a traveling companion. "You know, I have never been to Europe," she told us. "Maybe I could come along."

I was slightly discomfited by the idea at first—on first meeting Jess a few years earlier, Mom had sized up the two of us and commented, "You two look exactly alike! Ugh, the height of narcissism!"

But she turned out to be a terrific traveler, with interests and pacing similar to ours. When she gazed up at the glories of the Sistine Chapel, she explained that the sore neck she got was not a problem. "I'm a bird-watcher," she reminded us, "and warbler season is much the same."

However, some of Rome's treasures proved disappointing to her. She felt shortchanged, for instance, by the lack of carnality she perceived in Bernini's sculpture of Pluto raping Proserpine: "That's not much of a rape. He ought to lose the loincloth and really get at it." A few days later, we put her on a Vespa in one of Rome's busiest squares, the Piazza del Popolo. Mom revved the engine cautiously and then roared off like a bullet train, alerting passersby to her rapidly approaching presence by cautioning them, in English, "Careful! Careful!" She nearly clipped two Asian boys.

———

I DROVE UP TO MASSACHUSETTS on a Monday. Mom had previously asked all four kids to come on Memorial Day weekend and help her clean out the house. Standing at the kitchen sink, watching me make us dinner, Mom said, "JP says she wants to come 'for closure.' What does she think she's going to close?"

"I don't know," I said. "I have a friend who always wants to close things, too, and I never quite get it. But I'm probably not the person to ask—I'm always leaving things slightly ajar."

Will called a few hours later from his son's house on Cape Cod. I picked up the phone.

"Henry Alford!" he said. "Revoltin' turn of events."

"Yes," I said, all awkwardness. "I'm . . . I'm so sorry about all this."

"Steer your mother in the right direction."

"I will."

Our trip to Mohegan Sun the next day did, indeed, seem to amuse and distract. At one point during the bus ride, Mom looked at all the white hair on board and told me, "Sometimes I think, Isn't this great of me, that I'm willing to spend all this time with these old people?" I smiled. Mom added, "You probably think I'll never be that old, don't you?" She was right. In my mind, she's perpetually in her early fifties.

The inside of the Mohegan Sun casino is all browns and oranges, with swoopy sheets of glass overhead; imagine autumn transformed into a novelty cocktail, and then imagine that you are drowning in that cocktail. We played slots as long as we could before opting for the warren of stores; we hit a bookstore, a Starbucks, some clothing stores, and the Old Farmer's Almanac store.

After about three hours, we were ready to implode, so Mom suggested we go outside and lie on a tiny swath of green lawn that was slowly being baked by the sun. I remembered taking a theater-directing class once and the teacher telling us that one way to portray youthfulness onstage is to have people sit on the floor. Looking at Mom now, I realized that part of why she has always seemed ageless to me is that she has no problem parking herself on the ground. She loves the earth—she spent four summers in the 1990s removing large rocks from under her lawn and then carefully but mysteriously filling these holes with water from a garden hose. "Why are you doing this?" I asked at one point.

"The lawn needs a drink after that kind of upheaval," she told me. I smiled tentatively in response, having been unaware of colonic-based lawn care.

Now Mom lit up a cigarette. I took off my shoes. I asked her what she'd been looking at in the bookstore.

"Oh, I was reading Oprah's advice for leaving your lover."

"What does she say?"

"'Do it.'"

A few minutes later, I pulled out my cellphone and checked my e-mail. My brother, Fred, had responded to the "Weird Plans" e-mail; I read his response aloud to Mom: "I will try to remain as combobulated as any man can. This sounds wrong on paper, but to each her own."

Mom said, "I don't think what I'm doing is wrong."

"No. But it's progressive and alternative, and to any traditional mind it might seem, as you yourself called your e-mail, 'weird.'"

"But why spend money when I don't have to?"

"Because one assumes you're hurt and angry."

"But I'm not. And, weirdly, I haven't cried during this whole thing. The closest I've come is the other day when a cop pulled me over. He said, 'Do you know why I pulled you over?' and I said, 'I'm speeding?' and he said, 'Yes, and you look totally dazed.' Then he said, 'You look like such a nice lady I'm going to let you go.' I almost cried."

"Well, then . . . I guess you're not hurt and angry."

"Will's been a damned fool. But I've been a damned fool before, too. He's my friend."

"As long as you're not trying to convince yourself that you're not hurt when you really are."

"I don't think I am. But if I am, then I'll move out. And my alternative now is what—move in with one of you kids? I don't want to do that to you."

———

THAT NIGHT, while we were sitting in the living room watching TV, Mom stood, walked over to the cabinet in which she keeps all her good silver, pulled out the drawer of silverware, put it in my lap, and told me to take whatever I wanted. She said, "I'm not going to be doing any more entertaining."

I felt too self-conscious and too surprised by the suddenness of the act to tap into my inner greediness. But as soon as Mom left the room, I started pawing the beautifully sculpted pieces of shiny silver. I took three serving spoons and a knife. I liked the idea that, in the future, I'd be honoring Mom whenever I ate a meal that was deserving of the good silver. Nostalgia: it puts ten pounds on you.

We awoke the next morning and breakfasted on oatmeal. As I was leaving, Mom hugged me and said, "I love you to bits."

{ 10. }

People disappoint you. Lovers disappoint you. But theatrical memorabilia stays with you, as long as you keep it under clear plastic."

These are the words of a woman who'd been married three times by the age of twenty-five.

These are the words of a woman who has twice been nominated for Academy Awards and who once prepared an Oscar acceptance speech that ran, "I want to thank my ex-husbands for deserting me and making it possible for me to be here tonight."

These are the words of a woman who has outlived many of her friends and collaborators, including Andy Warhol, Zero Mostel, and Tennessee Williams.

These are the words of a woman who jokingly refers to her memorabilia-drenched apartment as a "museum" and to herself as the apartment's "gatekeeper."

These are the words of actress Sylvia Miles.

———

I'D MET SYLVIA MILES at a crowded party about fifteen years ago and had been impressed by her intelligence. She's prone to good anecdotes and to truisms such as "The establishment selects the avant-garde." I'd talked with her once on the phone after the party and then lost touch with her. But soon after I started on my quest for elder wisdom, I'd called her. Her statement about theatrical memorabilia bespoke an interesting take on the theme of self-preservation.

"Of *course* I remember you!" she shrieked, her excitable, interborough voice a veritable welcome-home sign. She suggested we could have lunch underneath the portrait of her that hangs on the wall of Sardi's, the restaurant in Times Square. I said great.

But when I called her a week later to remind her of the plan, Miles had changed her mind: "No, not under the portrait. *Across from* the portrait. That way we'll see it better."

MILES WAS WAITING FOR ME when I got to the restaurant at noon. If it is the actor's business to make a strong impression on others, then this Manhattan-born and -bred hot tamale can be said to be a consummate businesswoman. You can't not look at her. On-screen, the engine of this dynamic is emotional intensity. Her best-supporting-actress nominations, for 1969's *Midnight Cowboy* and 1975's *Farewell, My Lovely,* were prompted by a combined nine minutes of screen time. After Maureen Stapleton saw Miles's riveting turn as a tough-talking kept woman in *Midnight Cowboy,* she told Julie Harris, "Isn't that amazing? They went out and found a hooker and put her in this movie!" We could all profit from occasionally cultivating the fulsome certainty of Miles's chicken-leg-wielding yenta in *Crossing Delancey* after she introduces Amy Irving to Peter Riegert. (Instructions: Remove right hand from leg of chicken. Suck delicious grease off right thumb and index finger. Announce, "A poifect match!")

In person, though, the engine of Miles's impression-making has more to do with her looks, voice, and clothing. I invoke the phrase "throaty Sambuca rasp." I invoke the phrase "ten pounds of gorgeous in a five-pound bag."

———

POSSESSED OF A VERY PALE LIONESS'S FACE that is highlighted by vivid lipstick and shoulder-length blond hair, Miles was turned out in an all-black ensemble that also featured sunglasses, a diamond pinkie ring, sparkly eye makeup, and just-north-of-cleavage décolleté.

The waiter asked if I wanted a drink.

"What are you drinking?" I inquired of Miles, looking at the dark-red concoction in front of her. Miles starts each day off by drinking a mimosa ("to take my pills with") and so can be said to have a certain authority on the topic of elegant quaffs.

"A bloody bull. It's a bullshot with tomato juice."

"I'll have that," I told the waiter.

"Somebody has to," Miles said.

———

WE TALKED AND ATE for two and a half hours, covering a lot of bases. Miles told me that whenever she ran into society doyenne Brooke Astor at parties, Astor would always ask where she bought her clothes. Miles told me that when a director once said to her, "Put it on the back burner," Miles had realized, "Of course—I can always reheat it later, when I get home."

When I told Miles about my mother and Will, we got onto a long thread about obsessive-compulsive behavior. Miles told me that she suffered from obsessive compulsiveness some forty or so years ago. Part of her mania was directed at playing chess, to which she claims she was "addicted." This became a problem for her.

"So I said, Know what I'm going to do? I'm going to make my art the obsession instead," Miles told me.

"How do you do that?" I asked. "How do you transfer the obsession from the wrong thing to the right one?"

"It's like turning a negative into a positive. I did it by realizing that the most fun I ever had in my life was when I worked. So the healthy thing was to work more. Romance was not going to be that thrilling. Three marriages. I didn't need romance. But I did need my work. I had to learn how to make that my obsession."

"Was that hard?" I asked, realizing that Miles had never had children, which must have, for good or bad, allowed her a lot of time.

"It wasn't *impossible*. It was like the doctor saying to you, 'Look, you're gonna be in fine shape but there's no way you can eat turkey, there's something in turkey that doesn't agree with you. You can give yourself a heart attack from that.' Don't you think you can live your whole life not eating turkey but having a lot of fun?"

"Yeah, but—"

"So find something you like better!"

That Miles's profession is one that requires other people to hire her must surely have made this task more daunting. Yes, you can read your way through Jane Austen or Henry James, as Miles has done between acting gigs, and, yes, you can write your own one-woman show, as Miles did in 1981.

But what about the rest of your life?

Miles has implicitly responded to the question by turning her own person into one of her best performances. Indeed, I sometimes have the impression that I am not her interviewer, not her friend, but her scene partner. At the end of our lunch, for instance, I turned my tape recorder off and Miles asked, "How did I do? I mean, compared with Harold Bloom?" This was my cue.

This orientation, too, seems to be at the heart of her social-izing. Miles explained to me that the reason she has gone out so much over the years is because "people need to see me to hire me."

"Really?" I asked. "Despite two Oscar nominations and lots of theater credits?"

"They have to see me."

But over the years, Miles has taken flak for being a fixture on the party circuit. While it is, indeed, true that Miles has added sparkle and color to her fair share of public events over the years, the media's interest in these appearances has helped obscure the fact that Miles has, theatrically speaking, done some heavy lifting: she spent two years with Jason Robards in *The Iceman Cometh,* and she was in the world debut of Jean Genet's *The Balcony.* Her appearance in 1972's *Andy Warhol's Heat*—in which she improvised most of her dialogue—was the first time a legit actress had starred in an underground film.

The socializing issue came to a head in 1973, when the notoriously bitchy and misogynistic theater critic John Simon—he once compared Liza Minnelli's face to a beagle's and another time called Kathleen Turner a "braying mantis"—wrote a nasty review of a play Miles was in called *Nellie Toole and Co.* In his review, Simon referred to Miles as "one of New York's leading party girls and gate-crashers."

So Miles decided to strike back. Miles went to a New York Film Festival afterparty that she knew Simon would be attending.

"It was at O'Neals' in the back room," she told me. "I was sitting and chatting cheerfully, and just as I looked up I saw him standing at the bar. He was facing me and talking to Bob Altman. So I went to the table and filled up a plate with steak tartare, coleslaw, potato salad, and cold cuts."

Then she walked over to Simon and dumped the food on his head, saying, "Now you can call me a plate-crasher, too!"

Miles said to me, "He called me a gate-crasher! How could I

crash anything? I was invited to everything! I was the Gwyneth Paltrow of the day."

The food-covered Simon lashed out at Miles, calling her "Baggage!" He said, "I'll be sending you the bill for this suit," to which Miles countered, "It'll be the first time it's been cleaned."

Miles explained to me that she had phoned the publicist of the O'Neals' event before going, to make sure that no photographers would be present. She didn't want people to think that she exacted her revenge for the publicity. She also told me that she thought Simon had been gunning for her because he knew that she had visited the city in Serbia that he hails from—Miles remembers its name as Glub-Glub—and that she thought it was a dump.

I asked Miles if she'd ever regretted the Simon incident. She told me that she thinks she might have gotten less acting work as a result of the incident.

"I would have liked to have worked more," she said. "But I've never regretted what I did."

I stared into Miles's steely eyes. I remembered once reading her quip, " 'Oh, look at her, she's outrageous,' they say of me. Well, better *that* than I should be in-rage-ous."

Miles interrupted my recollection, saying, "My *reputation* is that I go out a lot. But sometimes I'll go into a grocery store, and someone will say, 'Look, there she is!' "

Miles told me that an important moment for her was the moment that she decided to be flattered by this attention—the moment she realized, "People think I'm at a party because I'm out of the house."

If you spend enough time being the life of the party, maybe you *become* the party.

———

AFTER LUNCH, Miles said she was going to take a bus home, so I walked her a half block over to Eighth Avenue. Miles has a bad knee, and whenever we walk on the street together, she wraps her arm around mine and holds on with varying levels of need, depending on her physical state. I find this highly endearing. "People are gonna think you're my nephew, airing me out for the day," she said to me once.

One time, when Miles's leg was particularly bad, she had me help her with a series of errands—I photocopied a drawing of her for some *Valley of the Dolls*–themed note cards she was making; I bought her the *New York Post* and the *Daily News* so she could look at the gossip columns. Then she wanted me to duck into her local grocery store with her. She warned me about the store's swift-moving mechanical doors: "You have to go fast through these doors. They're strong. I've gotten caught in them."

Standing in front of the store, I looked at said doors in action. Indeed, they exerted a military dictator–strength bluntness.

But Miles and I summoned our courage, took each other arm in arm, and made a dash for it.

We entered victorious.

Just inside the store's entrance, we found a tall shelf of jams and jellies. Miles pulled down a jar of Sarabeth's Kitchen strawberry-rhubarb preserves. She handed it to me, saying, "Open that for me, will ya?"

"Uh, sure," I said, looking nervously left and right for signs of employees who might not take kindly to my inspection of their goods.

As I stealthily started to twist open the top, Miles explained, "You have to open them to see if someone like me has already opened them."

———

AT THE TIME, "You have to open them to see if someone like me has already opened them" struck me as being absurdist, along the lines of Yogi Berra's "Don't always follow the crowd, because nobody goes there anymore. It's too crowded." But over the months, I've come to decide that Miles probably *has* opened and returned to the shelf a number of jars of jam, and so maybe this unusual shopping ritual is less absurd and more crazy-like-a-fox. The Miles conversational canon is full of such canny survival stories—like the one wherein a former boyfriend of Miles's who loved to clean bought her a somewhat elaborate, futuristic-looking Miele vacuum cleaner. " 'I'll show you how to use it,' he told me," she said, "and before I knew it, he had cleaned up the whole apartment. He said, 'Now you know how to do it.' So I said, 'But I think I need a few more lessons.' "

While Miles's offscreen persona is rooted in a worldy confidence—once, at a restaurant she eats at often, I handed her a menu, and she waved it away, saying, "A lover knows how to love, and a rapist knows how to rape"—but there's another side to her, too, one that's more introspective and seemingly mystical than her demeanor might suggest. One time, having fallen out of touch for a while, she called and told me she'd recently had a very quiet couple of weeks. "When I'm evolving, I tend to want to be quieter, not running around so much," she said.

"And what do you think you're 'evolving' into?" I asked suspiciously.

"I have no idea. But I'm not going to force it."

"Do you have any thoughts at all about what this new state might be?"

"What's that book about the states of your life? By the woman?"

"*Passages?*"

"Yes. It's more like something from *Passages*. I can always tell when I'm cleaning myself out, making room for the new thing . . . I seem to be looking forward to something. Whatever it is that's coming, I just have to make room for it, and it will come on its own." A beat. "I hope it's not a node."

———

I WANTED TO SEE THE APARTMENT. I craved the apartment. We'd always met at restaurants or theaters before. Miles carries press clippings with her wherever she goes—she's shared them with me, or should I say sicced them on me, a couple of times—but, memorabilia-wise, her one-bedroom overlooking Central Park is command central.

So we made a date.

Came the day.

When I stepped off the elevator on her floor, I was surprised to see Miles standing outside her door.

"The reason I came out here is to warn you," she told me slightly ominously. "It's *dense* in there."

She opened the door, and I stepped gingerly into a dark, cluttered vestibule that afforded views of the living room and kitchen.

I saw what she meant about denseness. Every wall, from floor to ceiling, was chockablock with posters, artwork, and photographs, most of them celebrating films or plays Miles had been in. The floor and the furniture were saddled with towering piles of *Playbill*s and magazines and props from movies; imagine a yard sale that is itself having a yard sale.

"You live in a Joseph Cornell box," I said. "Who dusts?"

"I do. Not frequently. I can't have anyone in because they would break stuff. And I don't entertain. There's no place to sit."

Starting in the vestibule—"That's the cover of *Rolling Stone* with me, Bob Dylan, and Dick Cavett," Miles explained. "We were at Mick Jagger's birthday"—we slowly made our way through the cryptlike splendor.

"That's Tennessee. That's Bob again," she said as we drifted into the living room.

Miles showed me how Andy Warhol wrote "Sylvia, I love you" on any prints he gave her. "There's a lot of love from Andy here," she said.

I asked if she ever "curated" the collection, and she said no but that sometimes she did throw stuff out.

"And do some things ever seem suddenly more important at any given time?" I asked.

"I can't concentrate on it. It's my life. I have to disassociate myself from it. If something's falling down, I'll move it. But I'm not connected to it anymore because I'd be obsessed by it if I were. My time—whatever time I have left, until I get an Academy Award—is for being an actor. I'm not retired."

When we eased into the kitchen, what had heretofore struck me as a charming decorative scheme now seemed claustrophobia making. Not only were the kitchen walls covered with memorabilia, but the counters, too, were host to tiny marching armies of action figures, photos, and tchotchkes.

"You only have a few inches of counter," I observed.

"I know. The collage is moving closer and closer to me."

At one point, as I was looking at the counter next to the refrigerator, Miles scooted past me, and I literally had to suck in my stomach lest I knock things over.

And then I did.

Just as we were going through some wooden, Western-style half doors at the end of the kitchen, I brushed against a five-year-old calendar featuring photos of celebrated New Yorkers, dislodging it from its peg.

It swooped, dead bird–like, to the floor.

Miles was slightly irritated. "I knew that was gonna happen," she said, bending over and picking the calendar up. "Unfortunately, nothing can be touched."

She carefully started hanging the calendar back on its peg. I reached out to help and she said, "Don't touch it. That's why I can't have people in here anymore. It's a museum. You have to think of this place as a museum. And in a museum you don't touch things."

I apologized profusely. I stood corrected, having previously thought the designation "museum" was a joke.

Eager to flee the scene of my cloddishness, I suggested we press on.

We exited the kitchen and walked down a tiny hallway.

Miles pointed to one of many photographs on the wall and said, "That's me and Shelley Winters. She's the fat one."

At the end of the hallway, I thought we were going to take a right, into her bedroom, but instead we proceeded straight, into the bathroom. Here, too, it was as if the walls had been decoupaged with memorabilia—the two citations for her best-supporting-actress nominations, a napkin with Elizabeth Taylor's lipstick smears on it, a picture of Jack Kerouac. I was conscious, in the confines of the tiny bathroom, of our shoulders touching.

"There's the mayor and me. Bloomberg," Miles said proudly.

"Right over the toilet: nice."

Just as I'd cast my eyes over the thronelike toilet seat—it's outfitted with a leopard-print pillow that rests against the lid—Miles turned and sat down on the commode. I smiled somewhat awkwardly, suddenly feeling as if the emotional stakes of our situation had been raised somehow.

Once comfortably seated, Miles reached about two feet in front of her and pointed at a clear plastic case hanging from the wall. Inside it was a three-inch-tall Andy Warhol doll, clearly a Japanese import. His minuscule head looked out the bathroom, in the direction of the hall. From her leopard-skin perch, Miles told me, "Originally, Andy was looking at me, so I turned him around so he's facing the other way."

When she pulled her hand away from the plastic case, I assumed that it would then make its journey to Miles's lap, where its partner rested. But instead, I watched the hand as it slowly snaked behind Miles's torso and proceeded to flush the toilet. Miles smiled puckishly and said, "There was nothing in there. But I thought I smelled something."

The tour ended in the bedroom, where we found Miles's elegant sleigh bed, over which hangs a Warhol silk screen of Marilyn Monroe.

"That's the most love I ever got from Andy," Miles said, explaining that the print is of the one that's hanging in the Museum of Modern Art. "And on the back is written, 'Sylvia, I love you.'"

————

WARHOL USED TO TEASE MILES for carrying her press clippings around with her. This fact is freighted with about seven thousand pounds of irony, given that Warhol's own shrewd sense of marketing once saw him silk-screening photographs of noted art collectors because he knew these people would shell out to acquire such flattering mirrors.

In a *SoHo Weekly News* column she penned in 1979, Miles explained her own motives for carrying around her mini-festival of self: "The handbag is the office, the factory, and the carrier of credentials and proofs of who you are when in motion and devotion to your career. I'd like to think that if I were put in a time capsule and found in the past or future, I would be the complete statement of the art, life, and times. Just a hard working girl trying to make a buck at art, as well as wearing and being it."

{ 11. }

Mom and I headed back to Durham for a long weekend. She'd been wait-listed at one of the finishing schools, but she wanted to find a temporary apartment to move into, as well as look at a few other retirement communities as backups.

Over the course of the three days, we looked at two apartments and two retirement homes. I was impressed, as I often am, by Mom's pithiness: seconds after she and Kendy and I were seated in a marketing director's or sales manager's office, Mom would open up with "I've left my husband and sold my house, and I need a roof over my head." Then she would say that she was looking for a two-bedroom unit on the ground floor. I could see that the salespeople loved this bluntness and specificity.

One of the finishing-school salespeople, a pop-eyed librarian type whose heavy southern accent transformed certain words into certain other words, told us that being able to help people in crisis situations was what made her job so "spatial." She calmly informed us that, as no "move-outs" were scheduled, she had no availability at present.

Mom said, "So it's a question of someone dying."

"Well, we hope they won't."

Awkward smiles all around.

We rambled around the four potential residences, imagining Mom as their inhabitant. In one of the units at the more luxurious and spacious of the two finishing schools, Kendy opened a closet door and excitedly trilled, "Ooooh, *this* is a closet to die for!" I stifled an explosion of laughter.

After the final visit, the three of us got some lunch at a funky gourmet store/deli called Foster's, where we sat on the porch. The porch has highly accommodating, weathered wooden furniture and is partially enclosed by lush climbing vines; you feel cozy and Adirondack, as if in the presence of moose.

We started talking about the relative merits of the places we'd visited and somehow got onto the topic of romance at finishing schools.

Kendy said, "You never know when Cupid's going to shoot his arrow."

"I'm not looking to attach myself to anyone," Mom said. "Men in their nineties are pretty used up."

"And dating in a community of only 150 people could get awkward," I pointed out.

Mom said, "The date would be you sit at the same table at dinner."

"It's like a date in the fifth grade," Kendy mused.

We had also been introduced, during one of the tours, to the concept of Nametag Night, when residents were encouraged to wear nametags at dinner.

"I bet that's a real help," I said. "Sometimes you forget a friend's name, but you're too far along in the relationship to ask again."

"Also, the activities director gives you ten dollars of funny money if you wear a nametag," Kendy enthused.

"I missed that," Mom said. "What's the funny money good for?"

"In-house auctions and maybe the gift shop," I remembered.

"Ooh, that's a fun way to pick up a little change for yourself," Mom said.

"And then the other way to pick up change, of course," Kendy added, "is when the residents die."

Mom and I looked at her slightly confused.

She explained, "Their couches."

———

WHEN I'D BEEN AT MOM'S HOUSE for the Mohegan Sun trip, I'd admired her album of wedding photos from her 1948 marriage to my father. Mom had brought the album down to Durham to give to me.

Because I did not know my father well—I was seven when my parents divorced and sixteen when my father died of throat cancer—pictures of him have always had a totemic pull for me, as if they'll solve the mystery of him. I mostly knew the late-period Fred Alford, the postclassical Fred Alford—a fun-loving guy who was spending a lot of time in ill-lit cocktail lounges, more or less waiting for his three-times-widowed mother to meet her demise so he could inherit. A husky fellow with a fabulous laugh, my father was a man whose animus was focused on eating and drinking and telling stories. I had the misfortune to spend a spring vacation with him in the late stages of his cancer, when a purple surgical scar on his throat was a bodily embargo on appetite, thirst, and anything more than a raspy quip. But Mom always talks about fun Fred Alford—Fred the raconteur, Fred the dancer, Fred the life of the party.

"Look at that button," Mom said as she and Kendy and I pored over the wedding pictures at Kendy's kitchen table one night. The button on my father's tuxedo shirt barely managed to keep his expansive belly at bay. "*Pzing!* It'll take your eye out."

I asked Mom to tell us about meeting our father. I'd never heard the whole story.

A vivacious, tomboyish girl from a well-to-do Minneapolis family, Mom was sent east in 1946 to attend a two-year's women's college outside Boston called Pine Manor.

"And was the nickname Pine Mattress used much then?" I interrupted.

"Not really. But it was a given that that's what nice girls did—went east and got married."

Shortly before the October freshmen mixer, a friend of Mom's told her, "I have the perfect person for you. He's a little short for you but otherwise great." My father was at a Stanford business-school satellite that had been started for GIs.

Mom told Kendy and me, "He had a car. A Lincoln Continental. Prior to that, all my dating in Minnesota had been done on buses—this was during the war, there was gas rationing—and often the guys were in parkas and mittens. So here comes your father in a Lincoln Continental, wearing a cashmere polo coat."

Kendy and I could sense her then-excitement.

"He had a Chesterfield. When he packed his suitcase, there were layers of tissue paper between his clothes. But the coup de grâce"—I'm here expecting to be told that my father stapled hundred-dollar bills onto my mother's bosom—"patent-leather dancing pumps."

Patent-leather dancing pumps?! Who *are* these people? I think. Yes, I knew that my father was a major prep, but *patent leather* on a first date? What's date number two—immerse self in mayonnaise?

Mom continued, "My mother sent me a pink strapless Ceil Chapman dress. Before the dance we went to a restaurant in Cambridge. I had chicken cacciatore."

Kendy and I nodded our heads—yes, yes, chicken cacciatore; nice.

"A week passes. Your dad calls me and asks me out on a second date. I say, You betcha. The afternoon of the date, a friend of his calls and says, 'Fred won't be coming, he got started a little early today.'"

"Perhaps a tiny clue?" I asked.

"I was hurt and disappointed, but, no, I had no idea what was going on. The next Saturday we *did* go out, to a club where Rudy Vallée was performing. I had a couple of drinks, probably among the first I'd ever had. By spring vacation, things were getting hot and heavy—we went parking a lot. He'd even pulled that 'I've run out of gas' thing. Then, at a certain point, he sent me turtles with my name on them."

"You mean chocolate turtles?" I asked, confused.

"No, real turtles."

Kendy asked, "Tiny or big?"

I suddenly have an image of my mother stacking five ancient sea tortoises in her dorm-room closet.

"Tiny. I put them in my bathtub."

I love it. Real turtles. The patent-leather desecration has been erased from my mind.

My father proposed that summer.

"I had an overwhelming feeling of 'This is how my life is gonna be,'" Mom said. "I said, 'Yes, absolutely.' Then I said, 'But I never want to iron shirts.' My family drove me back to Pine Manor from Minnesota the second fall, and on the way we stopped in Connecticut and visited Dad and his mother and stepfather."

Mom finished her second year at Pine Manor, and she and my father married that June.

"My father told me, 'Fred's a great guy, and you'll have a lot of fun with him. But there are going to be two problems. He's not smart enough for you. And he drinks too much.' Bingo."

I asked Mom when it dawned on her that Dad's drinking might be a problem.

"Immediately," she said. "But there wasn't much understanding about it. I spent a lot of time covering it up. We would come home late, and if he couldn't find his key he'd smash a window."

My parents set up house in New Haven but lasted less than a year there. My father worked a series of jobs at various of his stepfather's companies but couldn't seem to keep any of them. Then he explained to Mom that he'd gotten a job in Stamford, working for another of his father's companies, and that he and Mom should move there because the commute from New Haven would be too long. So they moved.

"But about a year into Stamford, I found out he wasn't working for his father."

"What was he doing?" I asked.

"I don't know. Not working. Sitting in bars was part of it. I remember asking him once what he'd been doing that day, and he said, 'Pricing Cadillacs.' I would say that that was the loneliest time of my life."

My parents moved back to New Haven—they'd had Kendy and my brother, Fred, by then and would soon produce little JP—where the gin and vermouth kept pouring. Dad had a party trick in which he'd balance a cocktail on his forehead and then lie down on the floor without spilling it.

"One weekend we went to some friends' house in Rhode Island. We drank, drank, drank. We were driving home to New Haven and started arguing about something, and I got so mad that when we stopped for gas a few hours from home and your father got out to use the bathroom, I drove home without him. He had to get a friend to take him home. Another time, after a party, your father, loaded, pulls out the car keys in the driveway, gets into the backseat of the car, and proceeds to accuse me of having stolen the steering wheel!"

Mom buckled at the waist with laughter. Kendy and I laughed pretty hard, too.

"This starts a *huge* argument, and I get so mad that later I get out of the car in traffic and walk the rest of the way home in bare feet."

I conjured up an image of my mother walking along the side of the road, her feet narrowly missing pieces of glass and bubble gum.

"So in the end—" I started to ask.

"In the end, the one thing Dad wanted from me was to be his drinking buddy. I tried and failed."

"Why did you fail?"

"I couldn't keep up. It got crazy. And kids deserve more than that."

My parents moved to Worcester, Massachusetts, in 1969—I was seven at the time—and divorced about a year later. Shortly before the divorce, Dad got Mom to sign a mortgage and then never shared the money with her.

"So you guys were married how long?" I asked.

"Twenty-three years."

"Interesting. Same as you and Will."

"You've heard of the seven-year itch?"

———

Driving back to kendy's house on our last day in Durham, we passed a fabric store at one point, and Mom asked if we minded stopping.

"Since I'm moving down here," she said, "I might as well get a dust ruffle for my bed and maybe curtains."

It seemed a little cart before the horse to me, but I gladly agreed to accompany Mom, eager as I was to be supportive. I'd brought to Durham what I later decided was the best-written piece of wisdom literature I'd read during my quest: Abigail Thomas's 2006 memoir, *A Three Dog Life*, about her experiences after her husband is hit by a car and suffers the rages and hallucinations of traumatic brain injury. One of the first things that Thomas does for herself toward the end of her grieving is go shopping, an act that prompts her daughter's comment, "Shopping is hope." So when Mom mentioned curtains and a dust ruffle, I thought she might be expressing Visa-based optimism.

I was slightly dreading taking a protracted tour of the store's thousands of bolts of fabric—am I alone in being semiterrified of the word "swatch"?—but just as I opened the store's door, Mom turned to me and announced, "I'm thinking a medium floral on a white background with just a hint of turquoise." The laser beam strikes.

———

LATER THAT DAY, the dust ruffle having been purchased in twenty-one minutes and forty-five seconds (not that I was counting), we found ourselves back at Kendy's, drinking tea and hanging out.

I was sitting at the computer and overheard a conversation between Mom and Kendy. Mom, her eyes beginning to well, looked up from her sudoku book and asked Kendy, "Do you think I'm being cruel?"

"No," Kendy said. She added, "But I'm on your team."

Mom tucked her pencil into the spine of her book and lay the book down onto the cluttered table. "I can get myself into such a dither thinking I'm abandoning him," she said. "But I've hung in there with him. And at my age . . . when you don't have a lot of time left, you have to do things faster. You . . . ."

Kendy reassuringly finished her sentence, "You get your dust ruffle and go."

{ 12. }

On the Sunday that I came home from Durham, *The New York Times Magazine* published a story by Stephen S. Hall that gave a good modern history of the study of wisdom. As an academic pursuit, wisdom studies are on the fringe of respectability, Hall explained. There's a lot of murk with wisdom, as it's so elusive. Does it mean decisive action or judicious inaction? Is it emotional or emotionless?

As a formal course of study in the modern era, wisdom can be traced back to the 1950s, when a young woman in Brooklyn named Vivian Clayton noticed that her father and grandmother, despite modest educations, exhibited unusual strength and problem-solving abilities in the face of adversity. At a time when gerontological research dealt only with the 5 percent of the elderly who lived in nursing homes, Clayton—a psychologist who studied at the State University of New York at Buffalo and the University of Southern California—took a wider view. She canvassed the canon of Western literature and came to the conclusion that although "wisdom" could mean a lot of different things, it was often applied to social situations and was marked by judgment, reflection, and compassion.

The notion that wisdom is about responding to social

situations was picked up by quantitative psychologist Paul Baltes, who'd followed Clayton's work. Baltes was one of the people who started the Berlin Wisdom Project in 1984, an attempt to "take wisdom into the laboratory." The project was built partly on research in which respondents were asked to respond to hypothetical vignettes such as "A 15-year-old girl wants to get married right away. What should one/she consider and do?"

According to the Berlin group, the wise response to this question would sound slightly tentative, with the respondee saying that marriage for fifteen-year-olds is not generally a good idea but that there are certain instances—if the girl is an orphan, say, or has a terminal illness or lives in a different historical period or culture than ours—when marriage might work out, depending on the girl's emotional state.

To some people, such a response might sound wishy-washy. But what I like about it is its sensitivity to cultural mores and situations. It also allows for a healthy margin of uncertainty and extenuating circumstances. The unwise response to the story of the fifteen-year-old, of course, is something along the lines of "She's an idiot to get married. It'll never work," which suggests an egocentric mind-set. So wisdom, according to this model, necessitates the ability to let go of absolutes when judging others and to consider their specific contexts. Interestingly, however, the Berlin group found, after running a battery of hypothetical vignettes on seven hundred people, that not a single respondent scored highly on all questions.

The most interesting part of the *New York Times* article— and the one that changed my ideas about wisdom—dealt with Stanford University's "beeper study." In 1994, Stanford professor Laura Carstensen and her colleagues gave two hundred Northern California residents, both young and old, beepers. The Stanford scientists then proceeded to beep the people at random times over the course of a week, sometimes five times a day, whereupon the people were asked to describe their emotional state. It turned out that the older folks had fewer negative emotions and were able to bounce back from their negative emotions far more readily than the younger respondees were. Moreover, the younger respondees' emotional states tended to be either wholly positive or negative at any given time, while the older folks were more likely to be experiencing a mixture of emotions. According to Carstensen, having mixed emotions helps regulate emotional states. It helps you to face the ravages of aging with a smile, for example. More specifically, the person who can appreciate the fragility of life is in a better position to savor it.

Serenity is, of course, a clichéd component of wisdom. But heretofore, when thinking about wisdom, I'd always been drawn more to decisiveness—be it Granny D's resolve about politics or my mother's about medium-size florals with just that hint of turquoise—than to emotional equilibrium.

But maybe wisdom is less a matter of certainty and action, I started thinking, than it is compassion that arises from coolheadedness. Maybe it's quieter than I thought it was.

{ 13. }

We four kids went to West Brookfield on Memorial Day weekend to clean out Mom and Will's house. We were to stay at a nearby motel while Mom and Will were at the house.

Kendy and JP went a week early, having sensed that Mom, who sounded pretty shaken, could use the moral support of her two daughters. We all knew that it would be staggeringly awkward to have Will still in the house, but we decided to do the best we could.

But by the time Greg and I showed up that Friday, Will and JP had already tangled and were hardly speaking to each other. If there's a do-gooder in the family, it's JP, who's a psychiatric nurse-practitioner and a pillar of her suburban community in California. She converted to Islam to marry the man she loves. She and Will have always enjoyed a lovely, tender relationship; Will taught her three sons how to fly-fish.

Kendy took Greg and me down to the lake and described what had happened. JP had shown up full of helpful suggestions for ways that Will could make his incipient Mom-less life better—Meals on Wheels, the town's senior center, et cetera—and Will, all doom, had snapped at her.

Kendy and JP and Mom had spent the week packing boxes and taking stuff to Goodwill. During the cleanup, JP and Kendy had found five of the mostly historical guns that Will collects. They proceeded to hide them.

My first sighting of Will occurred about two hours after I'd arrived. He was sitting at the top of the stairs (his bedroom is on the second floor), in total darkness. I could not see his face.

"Hi, Will. How are you?"

"Don't ask that question," his voice emanated from above.

"OK."

"Say, I have a question for you, Hen. I have that phrase from Shakespeare running through my head—'the slough of despair.' I'm wondering if it's 'sloo' or 'sluff.'"

"I think it's 'sloo.'"

"It's 'sloo,'" Greg, standing nearby, corroborated. "Sloo of despond."

About a half hour later, Will had worked his way down to the kitchen table. He started talking to me about the divorce and said, "This is the hardest thing I've ever been through in my life."

"I'm so sorry," I said.

"I'm much more depressed than I was the last time I saw you. That other time—you could show that interview to a psychologist and he would say, 'That's a classic case of someone who doesn't know how depressed he is.'"

"I think you knew."

He shrugged his shoulders and looked down at the floor. He said, "There's no animosity between us. And sometimes there's even a kiss good-night."

———

I DROVE MY TWO SISTERS and Greg back to the motel that night. JP told us that she'd twice asked Mom if she wanted to spend the night there, too, and Mom had said no both times. JP and

Kendy felt like Mom was not expressing, or perhaps not even grasping, the magnitude of her emotional turmoil. Mom had originally nixed JP and Kendy's plan to come early, but when they arrived, Mom and the house were wrecks, both much in need of minding.

"Well, you asked her twice," I said, turning the car off. "So she could have come."

The ominous silence from the backseat made me realize that I had not addressed the entirety of the situation.

"Will is not going to shoot Mom," I said. "He might try to shoot himself, but he would never shoot her."

"No, I don't think he would," Kendy said.

JP stared at the back of the driver's seat and said, "I just wish she'd come with us."

———

THE NEXT MORNING, in the basement, I was wrangling a particularly heavy filing cabinet and chair—my family seems to specialize in furniture from a period I think of as Early Courtroom—when Mom said to me, "Save that for Fred. I'm angry at him because I haven't heard from him for a couple of weeks."

Just then we heard footsteps coming down the stairs: my brother sporting a navy-blue T-shirt emblazoned with the words "ATF AGENT."

"Speak of the devil!" Mom said, hugging him. "I was just saying how mad I am at you because I haven't heard from you in my time of need."

Fred, our ironist: "I didn't want to overwhelm you with sentiment."

———

MY MOTHER IS A HOOKER. I mean, she hooks rugs. At her peak, slides of three of her rugs were shown during a lecture at New

York City's Museum of Folk Art; none of Mom's preshow statements better conveyed her excitement than the one that ran,
"Hookers are busing in from all over New England!"

And so today's highlight was the distribution of the forty or
so hooked rugs that Mom has made over the years. We spread
these treasures over the entirety of the wooden deck behind the
house—there were skinny runners with elaborate geometric
figures dancing about; four-by-five-foot ones covered with historical scenes and house fires and battalions of villagers; and a
two-by-three one featuring two crones sitting in rocking chairs,
surrounded by a border reading, "The Enduring Elegance of
Female Companionship."

We kids drew lots to see what order to pick our spoils in. I
drew third, and I bagged six beauties.

What intrigues me about my mother's rugs are the borders—usually three or four inches wide: she likes to do a complicated succession of very colorful zigzags such that you get what
you least expect in the earthy and highly traditional fiber arts:
psychedelia.

After the rug-off, we all agreed—corroborated by JP's experience working at a methadone clinic—that if Will were to
"act out," the moment would come when Mom and the movers
pulled out of the driveway ten days hence, when none of us kids
was planning to be around.

"I wish someone were going to be here with me," Mom
said.

Fred rose to the bait: "That sounds like a job for an insensi-
tive man."

———

THE CLEANUP had gone faster than anticipated. By Sunday morning
at 10:30, we were done, and everyone was eager to hit the road.

Will had bought a lot of clam chowder, which we had intended to eat for lunch on Sunday, but suddenly we all wanted to escape the doom of the house. It felt weird not to eat together, but then again, Will hadn't bothered to show up for any of the other meals that weekend, so maybe, we thought, it wasn't such a big deal. Will told Fred to take the chowder to Fred's house, where some of us were headed.

I didn't see Fred and Kendy say their final good-byes to Will—one can bear only so much emotional intensity in one weekend—but I happened to be in the kitchen during JP's. Standing about twelve feet away from him, she waved at him and said, "Bye, Will. Take care of yourself," and then turned to leave.

"JP! JP! JP! Come here!" Will wheezed with as much raspy volume as he could manage. "I just wanted to tell you that I found a fax that you sent me a while back that you signed, 'Your loving daughter.' I cried about fifteen minutes when I got it. I just wanted to say that if I hurt your feelings in the past couple of days, I'll always remember that note and that that's what you'll always be to me. I hope I'll see you again or talk to you again, and of course I'll be leaving some of my fishing rods to your sons."

"OK," JP said, her eyes brimming with tears. "Take care of yourself."

She turned and went outside.

I walked over to Will and hugged him good-bye. He was all rib cage.

"OK, Hen," he said. "Enjoy the chowder."

PART
TWO

{ 14. }

I met Charlotte on the high seas. We were dance partners.

I was writing a travel article about a seminar cruise to Alaska that the lefty magazine *The Nation* was hosting. When you put 460 of our country's more left-leaning citizens aboard a Holland America cruise ship, you get hundreds of instances of cultural dissonance—think a self-identifying "atheist social-ist Quaker" marveling at an ice-carving demonstration; think Birkenstocks in the piano lounge. "Do you think we'll ever see Ralph Nader in the hot tub?" I asked a fellow cruiser at one point, referring to one of the cruise's scheduled speakers.

"I don't think so," he told me. "Every time I've seen him he's disinfecting himself at the Purell hand-sanitizer station."

But none of these instances proved more memorable to me than the one I witnessed at dinner the first night of the cruise. On reaching my assigned table, I sat next to Charlotte, a tiny, attractive feminist and psychotherapist in her early seventies. Wearing a T-shirt that called for the impeachment of our president, Charlotte was instantly recognizable as whip smart and highly opinionated. She has a high, slightly Kewpieish voice that can quaver with conviction, like Lisa Simpson on a peace march.

During dessert, a discussion about Israel among the five

Jews at the table—two couples traveling together, and Charlotte, who was traveling alone—became heated, with the two couples disagreeing with Charlotte. At one point Charlotte asked the woman seated across from her, "Are you stooping so low as to call me an anti-Semite?"

The woman responded, "Yes, I am."

Whereupon Charlotte fired back, "Well, fuck you!"

I was too startled to speak, but the host of our table, Gary Younge, an Englishman who is a columnist for *The Nation* and *The Guardian*'s U.S. correspondent, nimbly defused the situation. The various parties scampered out of the dining room, muttering and shaking their heads in disbelief. Younge asked Charlotte if she'd like to get a cup of tea. Charlotte, still a little rattled by the incident, said, "What I'd really like to do is go dancing." So he escorted her up to the Crow's Nest—the immense, airy cocktail lounge on top of the ship, surrounded on three sides by windows—where they danced. When I found them a few hours later, I cut in.

And so our dance partnership was born—forged, as all the best ones are, in the crucible of political invective.

―――

THE NEXT TWO DAYS of the cruise were devoted to seminars. Various *Nation* writers, along with speakers such as Nader and Richard Dreyfuss, spoke on topics ranging from the 2008 election to prison reform to single-payer health care. The seminars were held in the ship's 867-seat auditorium, the Vista Lounge. Charlotte always sat close to the stage and asked a lot of good, tough questions; during the Q & A after a panel on the Supreme Court, she mentioned that all five conservatives on the Court are Catholic men, a point for which she subsequently received kudos from other passengers.

Gradually, word of the "incident" filtered through the 460

Nation-ites; at one point, Charlotte found herself in an elevator with Hamilton Fish, the former publisher of the magazine,
who told her that she was famous. Charlotte told me she'd
received lots of "You go, girl!"–type comments, as well as the occasional stare; but the latter may have had something to do with
the stylish and dramatic Susan Sontag–like streak of purple in
her otherwise black hair. And one day, the purple highlight was
showcased atop an all-purple clothing ensemble. When Younge
asked Charlotte about all the purple, she mused, "Well, purple
is the color of hysteria. And I'd say I'm 80 percent hysterical and
20 percent obsessive-compulsive."

On the third night—we'd embarked at Seattle, spent a day
at sea, and now had just spent the day in Juneau—a theme that
had been established the first night now reasserted itself. When I
casually mentioned "my boyfriend back home," one of my table-
mates—an oddball southern rancher of a certain age—started
discoursing about "the queers," causing another tablemate to
stand and flee the dining room in a huff.

"Are we getting too deep for you?" the oddball asked.

"*Deep!?*" the woman, a heretofore placid Southern Califor-
nian in her early fifties, shot back. "More like too offensive!"

An hour later, up in the Crow's Nest, I told Charlotte and
Younge about this new "incident." Charlotte suggested we throw
the queer-baiter overboard "and make it look like an accident."

Younge said, "You should have bent him over his chair and
skewered him."

Charlotte's and my turns on the dance floor that night suddenly seemed imbued with meaning. And vigor. On the preceding nights, we'd met the live band's steady burble of Motown
and Top Forty hits with a lively pageant of sashaying and shim-
mying, but now we went for broke. We danced the dance of the
oppressed. Charlotte piloted her thin five-foot frame with remarkable aplomb; in an exaggerated march step, she swung her

fists up to the level of her head and her knees up to her waist. We didn't need to wear berets; the berets were implied.

———

OVER BREAKFAST on the last day of the cruise, Charlotte—who's been married three times and has two children and four grand-children—told me that the man she was currently dating was going to pick her up at the dock in Seattle. They were going to go camping. She said that she had met him through a personals ad she placed in *The Nation*. I asked her if she'd come on the cruise hoping to meet someone. She said no, cruises mostly at-tract couples and widows; however, the *Nation* cruise that she'd gone on the previous year had led her to believe that its reader-ship might be a good place to "cast my net."

I asked more questions, trying to carefully walk the line be-tween interested and nosy. She told me that, in fact, she had placed *two* personal ads. The first had been a response to some-one else's that had bothered her. This ad had read, "Recovering fancy lawyer, 67, Shaker Heights, Ohio, seeks progressive female companion, 35–55, for cultural and social events."

"I was so angry about the young age," Charlotte told me, "that I called the *Nation* advertising person and asked, 'How can *The Nation* run an ad that's so sexist?' He said, 'We don't censor the ads.' So I said, 'I bet if it were a racist ad, you'd censor it.'"

So Charlotte decided, as a kind of test, to run the same ad but to switch the genders and the city ("Recovering fancy lady lawyer, 67, San Francisco, seeks . . ."). And, while she was at it, she figured she might as well run a real ad for herself.

"And . . . ?" I asked excitedly, knowing that she had at least received a response from the man she was going camping with.

"I got a ton of responses for my real ad," Charlotte explained. "But only prisoners responded to the lady-attorney one."

———

OVER THE NEXT FEW WEEKS, Charlotte and I talked four or five times on the phone. I called her the first time to interview her for my article, but the other calls were simply to chat. During our first call, I asked her what her favorite part of the cruise had been, fairly sure that she would mention either our dancing or her star turn during the Supreme Court panel. But no. She told me, "It may sound peculiar, but my favorite part of the trip was saying 'Fuck you' to that woman. I've been in conversations with these kinds of people for years and always had to bear their scorn. I've never had the courage to talk back. This was my opportunity. And I took it."

I also learned that the camping trip had not panned out as Charlotte had wished. Despite her personal ad's call for a "sexually active" gentleman, Mr. Camping had waffled in the trenches, telling Charlotte he "didn't know her well enough."

Charlotte told me, "Women my age are wise not to expect a twenty-year-old in bed and to be patient and caring and considerate of the difficulties men have at this age. And the men are wise to accept that they will never be twenty or even thirty or forty or fifty again and resign themselves to the aging process and get a prescription for Viagra when it's clear that it is necessary. Many couples just forgo sex, and the women sometimes couldn't care less, especially if they're not taking estrogen-replacement therapy. I have on several occasions said to the man that Mother Nature did not really want men to become fathers at seventy, when they could no longer provide for their children, just as she did not want women over fifty to become mothers."

You know how you meet someone on a trip who fascinates or delights you, and you exchange e-mail addresses and phone numbers and swear up and down that you'll get in touch, and then, fifteen years later, you find a little balled-up piece of paper with a mysterious name on it and think, "Who the hell is Pat F. Wonkman?" I thought Charlotte might be a Pat F. Wonkman. But I didn't want her to be. And so, seven weeks after the cruise, I went to San Francisco and spent two nights at her house there.

———

I WASN'T SURE what to expect. It struck me that a person as outspoken as Charlotte might be solitary and that her life might have large patches of darkness, the result of burned bridges. But there was much evidence to support the opposite conclusion. Charlotte lives in a lovely two-story house in Richmond, a neighborhood near Golden Gate Park. Her house is filled with artwork by and pictures of her four grandchildren; their handprints are pressed into the concrete of the patio and garden area behind her house, where we ate breakfast. Her phone rings frequently. She was dating a man named Felix, whom she'd seen the last four weekends. And her e-mail account—which sometimes receives as many as fifteen messages a day from the activist group Code Pink, with which Charlotte is active—appears to be the epicenter of the World Wide Web; having been away for the weekend before I arrived, Charlotte showed me that she had 826 unread e-mails.

Indeed, to spend time with Charlotte Prozan is to share her copious media diet. She's a religious reader of *The New York Times, The New Yorker,* and *The Nation*; she listens to NPR at a volume so bracing that you can literally hear it from her sidewalk. One day I opened the front door just at the tail end of a live opera broadcast and was met with a burst of applause so galvanizing that I instinctively bowed.

Charlotte is semiretired now and sees only three patients per week. Currently, her life is centered around the five classes she is taking at the Fromm Institute for Lifelong Learning, the school for seniors at the University of San Francisco. Charlotte arranged for me to go to two of her classes and then, on my last day, to interview Robert Fordham, Fromm's executive director.

On our first night together, Charlotte wanted to watch back-to-back episodes of Ken Burns's World War II documentary, *The War*. It sounded like a lot of mortar and talking heads to me, but I agreed. First, though, we ordered in some Indian food and settled into her cozy living room.

I wanted, of course, to talk about "the incident" on the cruise. Gently scooping a spoonful of curry and putting it on my plate, Charlotte told me, "One of the nice things about being old is that I don't care about being popular anymore. It's a tremendous freedom. I feel freer than I've ever felt before. My kids are raised, my parents have died, I've published three books, I have more time to read, I have a small practice, so I can travel. I feel smarter than I ever have. I think it's because I have so much time to read now."

Charlotte told me that her mind was blown two years ago when she read historian Chalmers Johnson's *The Sorrows of Empire: Militarism, Secrecy, and the End of the Republic*. "Previously, I thought I was well-informed," she said. "But I had no idea the extent to which the Defense Department runs the government."

Johnson makes the point that the United States has military bases on every continent except Antarctica, and these bases are a new form of empire. When Charlotte finished the book, she asked various friends and colleagues how many military bases they thought the United States has. Most people said about two hundred, but the actual answer is more like one thousand. They're in 153 countries.

"And then he shows you how the war machine is tied to the economy," she said. "Like how the Defense Department, on the eve of the war in Iraq, ordered 273,000 bottles of Native Tan sunblock."

We then proceeded to watch about four hours of *The War*. Throughout, Charlotte peppered the proceedings with fascinating tidbits: "Did you know that, with the exception of the

Northern California chapter, the ACLU went along with the de-
portation of the Japanese during the war?" "Niall Ferguson writes
that if we had made a preemptive strike against Hitler we might
have avoided the war. In 1939, the U.S. and Britain were militarily
superior, but we gave Hitler a year to prepare." "The government
set up day care for working women during the war. The Rosie the
Riveters. But when the war was over, the women were sent back
home so the GIs could have their jobs back. When women were
needed to work, they did, but when they wanted to work on their
own, they were pushed aside for the GIs. And is there day care for
them now?"

I found Charlotte's commentary fascinating, but between her
and the documentary and my jet lag, my head was starting to
swim, so I begged off and went to bed before the second episode
had concluded.

The next morning, Charlotte and I dined out on the sunny
deck, and, for reasons unclear to me, I was reminded of George
Bernard Shaw's remark that marriage is "an endless conversation at the breakfast table." I can easily imagine having a lifelong
conversation with Charlotte over a breakfast table, but it is less
easy to imagine this conversation if it has to be in competition
with the Iraq war. I asked Charlotte if she'd mind if we turned
the radio down a little, as NPR's coverage of that particular crisis, so hard on the heels of *The War*, was making me feel like I
was wearing a flak jacket.

Charlotte nimbly stood, walked into the house, and turned
off the sound. The relative quiet was lovely. When Charlotte returned to the breakfast table, I asked her, "Are you ever tempted
to tune out the atrocity?"

"No," she told me, "I can't get enough. I have seen every documentary about the Iraq war. I'm obsessed with it. I was young
during World War II. I remember the air raids, then the cold war
and the Korean War. The Vietnam War was very disturbing to

me—we were slaughtering thousands of men and women. My self-analysis as to why I'm so determined to protest the war is: all those stories about Germans who said they didn't know what was going on with Hitler. If my grandkids ask me, 'What did you do about it?' I'll have an answer."

I nodded.

She added, "If the Germans opposed Hitler, they'd be shot. But no one's going to shoot me."

———

CHARLOTTE IS A SELF-DESCRIBED JEWISH ATHEIST. Her atheism came to her shortly after the war, when she learned what had happened to the Jews in the concentration camps. "I had been raised with this mythology that the Jews were chosen people, and it just didn't compute," she told me. "I've never swayed. But I didn't talk about it much."

But in the past three or four years, her anger at the "Christianization" of the Republican party has caused her to call herself a "radical atheist." Which is to say, she's happy to talk about it with anyone who'll have a thoughtful dialogue with her.

What's interesting to me about Charlotte is that she's so fiery and opinionated on social issues, but when it comes to the individual she's utterly nonjudgmental. I didn't reveal to her that I was writing an article for *The New York Times* about the cruise until the last day of it, and Charlotte had no problem with that. She had no problem with my being gay and asked if I wanted to bring my boyfriend to stay at her house. She was unflapped by my request to turn off the radio during breakfast and by my subsequent intimation that her media fixation was overkill. Granted, I am, as her interviewer, in a privileged position. But Charlotte's cabinmate on the cruise had told me that Charlotte had explained a lot of political terms and theory to her without making her feel dim.

I could see why she'd make a good therapist.

Indeed, on our second night, we were having dinner at a terrific Burmese place called Burma Superstar, and Charlotte asked me, "How did your mother's divorces affect you?"

"I think I was too young—six or seven—to understand the first one. But this second one has been really upsetting."

I stared down at the table, trying to avoid looking Charlotte in the eyes. Suddenly taking note of this dodge, I tried to redress it by offering more: "I guess I feel like I've never had a strong father figure in my life, and that's probably why I shy away from male authority figures as much as possible. I like the ladies."

Charlotte smiled.

I asked her about her marriages. Charlotte's first husband left her when their children were five and thirteen, and she got no financial support. "I really had to work hard," she said.

"And were you wary of getting married again?"

"Yes. I didn't get married for eleven years. I was wary of myself. I thought I would repeat the pattern. But when I think of what I was like as a wife then, I think I was such a fool—so √ subservient."

But even the most stalwart individualist sometimes changes her mind: Gloria Steinem famously said she'd never get married or have children, but got married at sixty-six.

———

I ASKED CHARLOTTE if she thought she was a better judge of potential mates now, and she told me, "One thing I'm better at noticing
· is a drinking problem. You can tell who the alcoholics are. They're the ones who refill their glass before their glass is empty."

In the throes of the breakup of her marriage, Charlotte and some friends started a feminist consciousness-raising group.

"We met for seventeen years," she said. "People kept asking, Isn't your consciousness raised *yet*?"

In *The Fountain of Age*, Betty Friedan argues that one of the chief spurs to feminism was the increased life expectancy for women: "What really caused the women's movement was the additional years of human life. At the turn of the century, women's life expectancy was 46; now it was nearly 80."

One of Charlotte's breakthroughs was spurred on by a man she dated for eight years, a leader of groups for male batterers. "As soon as he heard about my three husbands, he said, 'All men are raised to believe that they are superior to women and they're entitled to receive services from them.' That was profound for me. It connected all three divorces. No one had ever said that to me."

Charlotte explained that her ex's job was to help batterers find different "mechanisms" for their anger, like taking a walk. "The violence occurs when the woman has not acknowledged the man's superiority or provided the services he thinks he's entitled to. The man strikes out to resuscitate his feelings of superiority," she said.

"And so how did your ex's statement connect your divorces?" I asked.

"I'd always analyzed my marriages on the basis of the individual characters of the three men. But one commonality, I now saw, was that none of my husbands could tolerate my disagreeing ✓ with them. It made me see that my disagreeing with them was an assault on their masculinity."

"Interesting that it came from a man and not from one of your feminist friends," I said. "Maybe that's why it struck you."

"After my third divorce, I asked a lot of couples the secret of their marriage. I was on a Sierra Club trip to Costa Rica and asked all the couples. I was surprised by how many of them had almost broken up. Someone told me his secret was 'Don't think you're going to change the other person. Accept them.'" Or leave.

AFTER DINNER, we walked across the street to a secondhand bookstore. We were excited to find one of Charlotte's books—*The*

Technique of Feminist Psychoanalytic Psychotherapy—on a table near the store's entrance. The book's cover features a somewhat dour black-and-white photo of Charlotte alongside her name in large type: Charlotte Krause Prozan.

Charlotte told me "Prozan" was her mother's maiden name.

"After my divorce, I wanted to basically move forward," she said. "Some of my feminist friends said that if I just used 'Prozan' as my name that that was still a man's name."

"So they wanted you to call yourself Charlotte Labia?" I guessed.

"No," she said, laughing, "they thought I should take my mother's first name and then add an 's' and '-child.'"

"What's your mother's name?"

"Mildred."

Charlotte Mildredschild.

I said, "Good save."

———

A HALF HOUR LATER, we found ourselves at the warm and brightly lit Jewish Community Center, where Charlotte had bought us tickets to a concert of Moroccan-Israeli music. After the show, we walked into the lobby, where platters heaped with apples and pastries were being summarily devoured by audience members.

Charlotte pointed out the Israeli vice consul and told me, "I had a very difficult time with the consul general of Israel at a lecture once. This was during the Lebanon war, and I was furious at Israel for dropping cluster bombs. I raised this point with the consul during the Q & A and said, 'You're murdering people.' After the lecture, I went up to talk to him some more, and he said, 'I don't want to talk to you, you said we were murdering people!' He got all huffy and walked away from me. He said, 'I don't talk to people who call us murderers!'"

Charlotte rolled her eyes heavenward and asked me, "Now what kind of diplomat is that?"

———

I WAS A LITTLE NERVOUS about my interview with Robert Fordham, which we'd scheduled for the last day. Over the course of my visit, Charlotte had recounted a couple of episodes that suggested her and Robert's relationship was not rapturous. For instance, at one point Charlotte had expressed interest in teaching a class and had been turned down. Also, Charlotte had voiced disapproval of the staff's hanging of a religious symbol—a mezuzah, donated by one of the teachers—in the school office's entryway. I knew that I'd want to ask him about Charlotte, and I thought this might be awkward. This suspicion deepened when the meeting ended up being held at a table in the school's lobby, with Charlotte in attendance. But both Robert—a big, tall, hearty man walking his shelter dog on a leash—and Charlotte behaved decorously.

I asked him why seniors crave education, and he said, "Not all do. They have learned its value. That lesson can't be learned later in life." I asked why the school had a preponderance of female students, and he said that older men did not like to assemble in groups. Charlotte asked why there were so many students with medical backgrounds, and Robert said that he wasn't sure but that Fromm was the best place in San Francisco to fall down.

When I asked Robert about Charlotte, he was candid: "Charlotte is one of our most dynamic students. She shows up wearing her world on her sleeve and on her chest. She has great passion. People are often criticized for being a bigmouth, but if you're passionate you have to speak out. She is extremely critical of shortcomings. She's looking for ways to rise above these shortcomings. We often disagree."

———

DIRECTLY AFTER THE INTERVIEW, Charlotte and I repaired to a Middle Eastern restaurant near the school, where we'd had lunch the previous day. We hunkered down at a table near a big window onto the street. After we'd talked about the meeting with Robert, I asked Charlotte a question I'd been wanting to ask since the first night I'd met her: "Do you think you pay a price for being so outspoken?" YES

"Well, I got called an anti-Semite," she said, tucking into a piece of spinach pie. "But it's worth paying." She paused before adding, "I'm sure some people think I'm an irritant. Like Robert."

Her self-knowledge struck me as admirable; most rabble-rousers' views of themselves are skewed.

It occurred to me, amid the food and the discussion about being outspoken, to tell her the story of how Sylvia Miles had dumped a plate of food on John Simon's head.

"Good for her!" Charlotte said, impressed. "Some people just say 'Fuck you,'" she added. "But now that I know about the plate of food . . ."

I took a discreet but firm grip of both of our plates.

———

SOMETIMES WHEN I TALK with Charlotte on the phone, her voice takes on the very measured tones of the health professional. I'm suddenly reminded that I'm talking to someone who's spent tens of thousands of hours talking to patients about their feelings, and I slightly fear hearing, "Okaaaaaay, that's all we have time for today."

Sometimes we talk about love. I remember once asking her what she thinks is the basis of most marriages' or relationships' failure. She pointed to people's inability to express needs. "There's a lot of fear around it," she said. "Fear that the other person will say, The hell with that. Most people don't have emotional courage. They play it safe, don't want to rock the boat."

"And do you think that as we age we get better at knowing what these needs are?"

— "Sure. But if you understand your needs better but are afraid of expressing them, it doesn't really help."

"And what about marriages or unions that *do* last? Do you see commonalities there?"

"It's important to allow for differences without having to be right. I was seeing a married couple for a while. They got along beautifully except for a sexual incompatibility—he wanted to have sex every night, and she wanted to have it once or twice a week. They kept blaming each other—'There's something wrong with him.' 'There's something wrong with her.' But neither is wrong, of course. They just have to compromise. Meet in between."

She paused then added, "It reminds me of that Ralph Nader–Robert Scheer debate we saw on the cruise."

Ralph Nader and the journalist Robert Scheer had had a fiery debate in which Scheer had accused Nader of helping Al Gore lose the 2000 election. Scheer had said, "There's no clearly defined third party. You didn't build anything." Nader preached the importance of having a third party and added that if the Democrats had embraced more progressive ideas like full Medicare and the living wage, Gore would have won the election.

Charlotte reminded me that her sympathies had ping-ponged during the debate; she'd been unable to decide which of the two men was right. She said, "If you go on the basis of principle, Nader is right. If you go on the basis of pragmatism, Scheer is right. There's that expression, 'Politics is the art of the possible.' Well, maybe marriage is the art of the possible. You'll never get everything you want. You'll never have every single one of your needs met. But what is possible?"

{ 15. }

It took me a long time to go visit Mom at her new digs. I made plans to go one weekend and then canceled; another time, I wrote down "Durham" on a to-do list and promptly lost the list.

At first I chalked up my inaction to my busy schedule. Then I told myself that I was letting Mom settle into her new life. But the more I thought about it, the more I realized that, in putting herself in a community of older folks, she'd forgone the transitional apartment, and gone straight to Croasdaile—Mom had now defined herself as old. I wasn't sure I was prepared for this. So much of my mother's and my friendship is dependent on, if not based on, her gameness.

Two summers ago, I went to Hawaii's Big Island to write a story about volcanoes for *Travel + Leisure*. I'd decided that it'd be fun if, after I'd spent three days tromping around Volcanoes National Park, Mom flew out and joined me for a couple of days of relaxation on the beach. She loved the idea.

I spent my three days in the park assiduously trying to get more and more proximate to hot lava. I went on a fairly terrifying five-hour hike one day, and I scrabbled over the craggy coastline one night with crowds of tourists—without ever actually seeing any lava flowing.

So, when Mom arrived, I arranged for us to take a helicopter tour that would take us directly over a volcano's active vent. I gleefully and slightly sadistically anticipated the juicily dramatic scene I would be getting for my story.

I told her, "There's something interesting about the helicopter." Mom raised her eyebrows questioningly. I explained, "It has *no doors*."

"That *is* interesting," she said, her expression betraying no panic.

Indeed, when we'd strapped ourselves into the craft—a tiny three-seater manned by a pilot named Joyce—Mom still seemed fairly steely. Meanwhile, I was starting to sweat: I was seated next to the open door and, due to limited space, all of my right shoulder hung outside the craft. To test my seat belt's strength, I started tugging on it with a vigor that seemed almost fetishistic. Some fifteen minutes later, as we hovered over the mouth of the volcano, the helicopter canted at a thirty-five-degree angle, the concentration that it took to pin my body back against my seat forbade any verbal communication other than a grunt of amazement at the volcano's eerie beauty. But Mom and Joyce carried on like a couple of old salts surveying a rippleless ocean.

Mom, seeing my panicked expression, asked if I was OK. I mumbled yes.

The helicopter continued to cant over the roiling lava.

Joyce said, "Don't worry, Ann—we won't make a human sacrifice today."

Mom: "Well, you wouldn't sacrifice him—he's not a virgin."

Would Mom and I still take trips like this? I wondered if her move to Durham wouldn't spell the demise of her kickiness. One oft-cited theory in aging studies is the disengagement theory, which argues that, at a certain point in their lives, old folks pull away from other people in order to make their ultimate departure less disruptive to the smooth functioning of society.

I worried that the yin of disengagement might be at odds with the yang of hot lava.

———

OR WAS MY HESITATION more deep-seated?

Over the years, my mother's actions have suggested that hers is the wisdom of the small scam. Growing up in Worcester, I used to accompany my mother food shopping at Iandoli's, the local grocery store. Iandoli's had a bakery on-site; you'd be pulling your box of shredded wheat off the shelf when suddenly the aroma of fresh, hot bread settled around you like a floor-length mink. So Mom started a delightful ritual: while we were shopping, we'd get a loaf of hot bread from the bakery, rip the packaging off a stick of butter, which we'd rest on the seat of the shopping cart, and then proceed to tear hunks of bread from the loaf and drag them through the butter. We could easily polish off a whole loaf and half a stick of butter as we strolled around the store.

I remember having two distinct thoughts about this activity. First, ThisisthemostfunthingIhaveeverdoneinmyentirelifeandmaybeonedayIwillgettoworkonanairplanewhereyougettopushfoodoncartsandsometimeseatit. And, second, Is Mom going to pay for the bread? There seemed to be some wiggle room here. Once, when we were a group of four shoppers, we'd gotten a loaf of bread *and* two cinnamon rolls, the latter of which were promptly devoured and then not paid for. The subversive nature of not paying was, to a ten-year-old, slightly terrifying. I would skulk through the checkout line and out to the car. Seldom has a car lock seemed such a relief.

About six years ago, when six of the Alford women went on a pampering vacation to Scottsdale—they called this trip, and themselves, "Spa Girls"—Mom walked off with a pair of slippers that she was meant to wear only in the spa. My sisters love to tease Mom about this, and you need only say the words "the slippers at Spa Girls" to one of them to describe a world in which expedience always trumps protocol.

I, for one, am enthralled by Mom's laser beam. She doesn't cut to the chase; she starts at the chase. *Did you think they were going to* wash *the slippers after each person has worn them? It's not a bowling alley.*

In recent years, I have tried to harness this unique energy of Mom's and to turn it into cold, hard cash. In 2003, we took another travel assignment, this time to Palm Beach to attend a "society soirée" package weekend sponsored by the Colony Hotel. The idea of the piece was that Mom and I, in the course of a weekend, would try to claw our way into Palm Beach society.

Unsurprisingly, the guests who attended the Society Soirée package weekend did not bear the last names Rockefeller or Du-Pont. However, early in the weekend, an eagle-eyed Mom made a poolside sighting of Dominic Chianese, who played the ailing gangster Uncle Junior on *The Sopranos*.

"Fabulous work, Mom!" I said. "He's no Mary Lou Whitney, but I'll take him."

So Mom sidled over to Chianese and chatted him up. Chianese is a lovely man—avuncular and warm, more monsignor than mobster. Mom proceeded to recite from memory a coruscating piece of Uncle Junior dialogue—"I've got the Feds so far up my ass that I can taste Brylcreem"—whereupon Chianese burst out laughing, and Mom waved me over. Chianese introduced us to his wife, Jane; we chatted for about ten minutes. As we were taking our leave, Chianese said, "God bless you." We loved it. We were *in*.

The next day, having also befriended the singer in the Colony's cabaret—a bluesy chanteuse named Baby Jane Dexter, who happened to be pals with Chianese—Mom and I found Dexter and the Chianeses resting poolside. So we dropped by to say hello. When Dexter tried to introduce us to Chianese, we said, "Of course, of course, we know Dominic," as if to suggest that our mutual roots reached back to trading bottlecaps on the playground of Bronx Science. Before we knew it, Dexter was taking a photo of Mom and me with Chianese. *Click. In even further.*

Mom and I jumped in our rental car and did some sightseeing that afternoon. When we pulled up to the hotel in the early evening, who should be sitting in front of the hotel but Chianese and his wife. Seeing us, Chianese looked slightly anxiously at his wife, and then the two of them immediately stood and *fled* into the hotel.

I started laughing.

"We may have overstepped the boundary on that one," Mom said.

"Unh, yeah."

And so, having not visited Mom in her new living situation and having had too much time to grow introspective, I found that a strange thought entered my brain: was Mom's divorce from Will her biggest-ever scam?

THE MORE I THOUGHT ABOUT WILL, the more I realized that the aspect of wisdom that he most has to grapple with is nonattachment. After all, what is addiction if not unhealthy fixation? (Carl Jung called addiction "a prayer gone awry.") Additionally, the divorce asked him to let go of a relationship that had been his mainstay for more than thirty years. Neither of these assignments in nonattachment could be easy, but when you curb your bad impulses, at least you have moral victory on your side. But accepting or coming to terms with your spouse's divorcing you is ungraced by the balm of moral victory and instead requires that you embrace another of Buddha's paradigms, that all life is in a state of constant flux. I told a friend the details of Mom and

Will's divorce, and the friend said, "Will is like an involuntary Buddhist." I could see his point.

―――――

I WANTED TO KNOW MORE about nonattachment in a Western setting, so I called Larry Merculieff, an Alaskan native wisdom keeper. In various civic and governmental capacities, Merculieff has spent almost four decades serving his people, the Aleuts of the Pribilof Islands. Merculieff is only fifty-eight, but, as he told me, being a Native American elder "doesn't have anything to do with age. It has to do with your ability to speak to people. I once met a five-year-old Athabascan elder. He knew four languages."

Merculieff told me that he started meditating at age five. You can't meditate well unless you are able to detach yourself from daily anxieties and preoccupations. "I was expected to sit on the shoreline hour after hour. It allowed me to tap into the physical planet—like being able to sense when an animal is coming. It allowed me to be present in the moment. You don't know what it means until you become a field of awareness."

Merculieff told me about standing under a flock of tens of thousands of birds and being powerfully struck by the realization that most of the birds had probably never clipped a wing or flown out of formation or even brushed up against one another while flying.

"The only way for these animals to live is to be fully present in the moment," he said. "I used that for the rest of my life."

―――――

AMONG THE EXTANT PEOPLES least touched by civilization are the Moken. The Moken, who number between one and three thousand, are nomadic tribesmen and animists who live in the Andaman Sea of Indonesia. With a primal understanding of the ocean that rivals any oceanographer's, the Moken are practically amphibious—they learn to swim before they walk, and they can lower their heart rates to stay underwater twice as long as we can. More interesting, though, is their concept of time—or seeming lack thereof. They have no words for "when," "hello," or "good-bye"; individuals don't know how old they are. Someone who has been absent from the tribe for fifteen years will be greeted upon his return as if he had gone to a neighboring island for a day or two.

I bring the Moken up not simply to show that there are people who exist using what has the shape and feel of animal intelligence but rather to show what this same intelligence can do: though their village and boats were demolished, all but one of the tribe—a disabled man, who was unable to run—survived the tsunami in 2003 that took hundreds of thousands of lives. It seems that, on the day of the tsunami, an elder Moken fisherman named Salama Klathalay noticed forebodings of trouble—the tide receded abnormally, dolphins headed out for sea, cicadas on the land stopped their buzzy singing. So he alerted his fellow tribesmen, and they all climbed up a local mountain.

{ 16. }

As our parents age and change, we may need to, too. My friend Sandra Tsing Loh, the writer-performer and NPR commentator, has written often about her father. Orphaned at age twelve, Eugene Loh is an eighty-seven-year-old retired aerospace engineer who left Shanghai to come to the United States for graduate school; he has five science degrees, including ones from Cal Tech, Purdue, and Stanford.

Over the years, Sandra has chronicled some of her father's more, shall we say, beguiling personal habits. This is a man who takes frugality to a very, very high level. When the elbows of his sweaters wear out, he simply turns the sweater around and wears it backward. For many years, his primary mode of transportation was hitchhiking, even though he owned a car. Any important documents that he needs to carry with him are stowed in a battered cardboard Golden Flax cereal box, which he carries in a plastic grocery bag he throws over his shoulder. He and his fourth wife— a tiny Manchurian sprite named Alice—harvest the better part of their diet from food they find in garbage cans and dumpsters.

I somewhat sheepishly asked Sandra one day if I could interview her father. I was sheepish because I would never want to be accused of turf stealing, and for many of us fans of Sandra's work the words "Eugene Loh" are inextricably linked with the words "comedy gold." But Sandra graciously agreed, handing over both his phone number and the message "Even negotiating his answering machine will be a rollicking journey for you."

———

Dr. and Mrs. Loh live in a three-bedroom ranch house a block from the beach in Malibu. This is surfer Malibu, not movie-star Malibu, about four miles north of where the glitterati are and surrounded by gorgeous, gently rolling hills, not guardhouses and shopping malls.

Loh bought the house for $47,000 in 1962, and it is looking a little down at the heel; note the tie-dyed tapestries flapping in two of the bedroom windows through which the Lohs' four boarders—two of them baristas at the local Starbucks—can be seen making their entrances and exits.

"Welcome, special guest!" Loh greeted me in his driveway. Stoop shouldered and strikingly handsome, Loh has bristly salt-and-pepper hair and a lot of energy. I'd asked him if I could tag along on his daily regimen of physical exercise down at the beach. Loh has a remarkable body for his eighty-seven years, and he performs a complicated series of stretches and flips on the beach playground's jungle gym.

At the house, Loh ushered me into his dining room, where we sighted three large clumps of mostly blackened bananas. He asked me, "Would you like a banana?"

"You buy so many at one time!" I exclaimed, still getting my bearings.

"We don't buy them," he explained. "They're from the dumpster behind the grocery store."

Oh, right. Somehow in my nervous scramble to prepare for this interview—did I want to wear my bathing suit under my pants for our beach visit or just carry it?—I'd forgotten about the dumpster diving.

Sure, I said, I'll take a banana.

"Wait a minute," Loh said. He then said something in Mandarin to Alice, who went to the kitchen and returned bearing a slightly less blackened—and of slightly more recent liberation from a dumpster—banana.

"Here," said Loh, handing me the speckled treasure. "You are special guest."

I FOLLOWED LOH to the backyard, where he unpinned his tiny Speedo—it's sky blue and covered with black leopard spots— from the clothesline.

"That's a very racy suit for a gentleman your age," I said.

"I took it from the men's room down at the beach. Someone left it behind."

We started on the four-minute walk to the beach club. Loh and his wife live in a planned community called Malibu West. For about $1,600 per year, Malibu West residents are entitled to join the club, a simple glass-and-brick pavilion on the beach, which offers showers and parking.

Loh likes to walk closer to the traffic than he might. He has painful bunions and tends to scuff his feet; he once told me, "When you're old, you're not walking, you're sliding."

"Uh, Dr. Loh, I'm gonna cling to the shoulder a little here because you're sort of walking in the road," I said at one point.

"OK," he said, undeviating.

Loh is highly social, and he waved and hallooed to various people he knew on our walk, once yelling out "Wie geht's?" to a fellow German speaker and "Inshallah" to a pedestrian who smiled indulgently at him. Loh has traveled and lived all over the world, including a three-year stint in Cairo, where he taught at the American University.

As we walked, I asked him how he had liked being in Sandra's work over the years, and he told me, "I'm very happy, of course. Some people say she makes fun of me, but if she didn't make fun of me, no one would make fun of me."

Over the years, life with Eugene Loh has posed its challenges for Sandra and her siblings. Once, when Sandra was in junior high and her father was doing a lot of hitchhiking to save money, he made Sandra accompany him to the dentist. Determining that the duo would get more rides if Sandra appeared to be a lone hitchhiker, Loh obscured himself behind bushes and put his young, insecure, teenage daughter out on the road alone, only to materialize once a car stopped.

Loh clearly enjoys the savings that hitchhiking affords. But there's another aspect of the experience that draws him to it as well: "When people don't give you a ride, you feel humility, you feel humble. When people give you a ride, you get excited, so in brief time you have a nice turn of emotions, like a small history."

Loh and I went through the beach club's metal gate, where we met the club's fortysomething Swedish manager, Ann. Ann asked me if we'd come through the gate, and I said yes. Her face betraying a certain amount of irritation, she said of Loh, "He used to climb the fence. He'd climb on the mailbox, and I had to threaten him with a shotgun. I don't want him on the mailbox."

I reassured her that we had not been on the mailbox.

———

Loh and I walked to the changing rooms in the building's basement, which were devoid of people. Saying, "Cheap Chinese man like to turn off the lights," Loh proceeded to turn off five lights.

We slipped into our bathing suits in semidarkness. Loh's

suit is a sop to the beach club, as he would prefer to swim naked; it looked like a necktie tied around his midsection and gave view to several inches of plumber's crack. Telling me that he had studied yoga and modern dance in the past ten years or so, he proceeded to do a series of breathing exercises, after which he exercised for a half hour on the beach and we plunged into the icy water.

"Cold water wake up old man!" he said as we walked back to the changing rooms.

I said, "Younger man, too."

A more reflective mood passed over us in the changing rooms. Loh asked me about my wisdom project, and I explained. I told him that my mother and stepfather's marriage had foundered. I said, "It's sort of a weird time in life to get a divorce."

Loh responded, "Alice takes care of me now."

I allowed as how Loh, now on his fourth wife, had had a lot of experience with love. I asked him if he felt like he was a better judge of potential mates as a result, and he told me, "Not necessarily."

I asked him what he'd learned about love.

"Your idea of love might depend on your age," he told me. "At a younger age, love is mostly about romance—Romeo and Juliet. In middle age, it is mostly about sex. In old age, you care for each other."

Placing his wet bathing suit on a diaper-changing table he'd pulled down from the wall, Loh shuffled over to the hot-air dispenser as he told me, "In your mother's case, don't worry. She can find someone if she wants to. When you're old, what you want is a companion."

Pressing the dispenser's button, he turned and put his bare bottom directly under the flow of air. He said, "Nice to have warm air there!"

———

SANDRA AND HER TWO SIBLINGS' MOTHER was German and died of Alzheimer's when Loh was sixty. Ten years later, Loh decided to find a new wife—specifically, a Chinese wife.

I asked him, "Why did you decide to remarry at seventy?"

"When you're young, your sexual drive is strong. I'm outgoing. So it's a very natural thing. Ingmar Bergman married many times. Doris Lessing married twice. I can't compare myself with these famous people, but we are all outgoing."

"And why specifically a Chinese wife?" I asked.

"It's like music," the amateur opera singer told me. "The German wife was in the key of G. German, G. I wanted to marry in my home key—C, Chinese. I've returned to China nine times, most times to try to find a woman."

If Loh's hitchhiking and penny-pinching and odd ways were difficult, if not traumatic, to his children when they were growing up— Sandra's sister was estranged from her father for eight years—his search for a new wife was near impossible. In her comic monologue *Aliens in America*, Sandra recounts the process of her father—whom she refers to in the piece as "Old Dragon Whiskers" and "the wily mandarin"—searching for a new mate at a time in his life when she says he was "starting to look more and more like somebody's gardener." Forged in fury but written with the clarity of reflected-upon rage, the piece is Sandra's finest work and can be said to have launched her career. It aired on *This American Life*, and the section titled "My Father's Chinese Wives" won a Pushcart Prize.

Early in the monologue, Sandra's sister posits her own theory about why their father was looking for a Chinese wife:

> You take an Asian immigrant off the boat . . . Here is a
> woman fleeing a life of oppression under a communist
> government and no public sanitation and working in
> a bicycle factory for ten cents an hour and repeated

floggings every hour on the hour . . . after that, living with our father might seem like just another bizarre incident of some kind.

Loh's marriage to his first Chinese wife was particularly rocky. After writing to his family in Shanghai saying he's looking for a wife, Loh got seven responses. ("I have to face the fact," the baffled voice of Sandra tells us as the résumés and head shots start trundling in, "that my father is, well, hot.") Forty-seven-year-old Liu Tzun was flown to Los Angeles; a week later, she and Loh were married. "The fact that Los Angeles is near Hollywood has not escaped her," Sandra tells us; Liu was revealed to have ambitions in the entertainment industry. But, because she spoke no English, Chinese singing was her "hook." In *Aliens in America*, Loh says to Sandra, "I know you have friends in the entertainment industry," to which Sandra responds, "He has never fully grasped the fact that most of the people I know do, like, hair for *America's Most Wanted.*"

Five weeks into the marriage, seeing only backward sweaters and cereal-box briefcases where she hoped to see Oscar statuettes and deal memos, Liu left a note for Loh on the kitchen table reading, "I have left you, Dr. Loh, and taken the Toyota— so there!" Divorce and a passel of lawsuits followed.

Chinese wife number two—thirty-seven-year-old Zhou Ping from the Qang-Zhou Province, who had worked in a Manchurian coal mine until she was twenty-five—was a better fit and was even able to bring Sandra's sister back into the family orbit. But not better enough to go the distance.

Which bring us to number three, lovely Alice, who is a dynamo of industry and affection and shows no sign of stopping.

———

AFTER THE BEACH, Loh suggested we stop at the Starbucks between the beach club and his house. Once on the cement terrace in front of the store, Loh walked up to a garbage can and started sifting through its contents. He removed the lid of a cardboard cup of coffee; seeing it empty, he threw it back in the can. The second coffee cup had two inches of milky coffee in it and a cigarette; Loh fished the cigarette out and then drank the coffee. Moving on to a second can, he found a three-inch butt of a baguette and, biting into it and meeting resistance, pronounced it stale. He threw it back in the can. But this second can held cups containing an inch of hot chocolate and several inches of a latte; Loh mixed them together and drank up, announcing, proudly, "Cocktail." Loh darted into the store, finding in a garbage can therein some uneaten slices of apple and a *New York Times,* both of which he put in his bag for later consumption.

I watched this process first in fascination, then mild embarrassment (there were five or six people sitting on the terrace), then slight irritation, then cool detachment. It was a rainbow of emotion for me—Elisabeth Kübler-Ross, for leftovers. I tried to imagine what it would feel like if I were his teenage or college-age son, and I knew that it would have caused me to turn inside out with embarrassment.

As we walked up the hill, I asked Loh if he ate food out of the garbage because he believed in recycling or because he likes the taste. He said that yes, he believes in recycling, and yes, the food he finds at Starbucks or behind the grocery store is often delicious, but mostly he does his dumpster-diving out of habit and because he was raised to be frugal. He added, "And the immune system is increased from this."

He told me that sometimes people who see him going through the garbage will, presumably thinking he's homeless, offer him money; Loh will pocket the money and continue diving.

BACK AT THE HOUSE, Loh took me into the garage, where we saw the motherlode. Spread out on shelves and a stacking system were foods that he and Alice had collected—I saw about twenty apples, twelve oranges, four heads of lettuce, and an entire watermelon. Then Loh opened the refrigerator and showed me three quarts of milk, several sandwich fragments, a few pieces of sushi, and lots of juice.

"*Milk?*" I asked, unable to stem my journalistic detachment. "Sushi?"

"Cheese is mold," Loh informed me. "In China, the soybean sauce is made from fermented soybeans. Wine is fermented grape juice."

"Unh-huh," I mustered.

———

ALICE SERVED ME A CUP of tea in the dining room. When I put my soggy tea bag on a spoon that was on the table, it leaked onto the table. Loh swooshed in with a napkin he'd liberated from Starbucks and said, "See? Old man may be weird. But very useful."

———

I SIPPED MY TEA. The afternoon light was caramel-like.

Loh asked me, "What happened with your mother?" I explained that my stepfather had problems with substance abuse. Loh sympathized with my mother, "No, she can't do that. It's too late." He paused and added, "Just like the stock market, you have to write off the loss."

I continued sipping my tea, and Loh asked me if I wanted to hear a radio piece that Sandra had just done for her weekly commentary on KPCC. I said sure. The piece, it turned out, was about how her father likes to eat food he's found in the garbage.

Loh closed his eyes while listening, and I couldn't tell if this was a sign of pain or rest or concentration.

"The line of appropriateness keeps getting pushed out further and further," Sandra's commentary ran. "In the Carter years, I was horrified by the dumpster-diving." But gradually, she explained, she has softened. She wouldn't go near the southwestern chipotle tuna tostada wrap that she saw her dad and Alice tucking into during one long car ride. But a rye bagel that's in pretty good condition? On a day when you're really hungry? Why not?

When the piece ended, Loh opened his weary eyes.

"So what do you think?" I asked.

"Nothing. I don't feel ashamed of it. She's written about it just like you will. She should be grateful. I supply her a lot of material. Maybe I should charge her."

When Sandra started performing *Aliens in America* onstage, her father wore a floor-length blue satin Mandarin robe to the opening and sat in the front row taking photographs and turning heads. (Said Sandra, "God forbid any attention might be focused on me.") After some performances, Loh would get up onstage and start miming Sandra's movements; audience members who had not yet exited the theater would see him and give him the standing ovation that they had usually not given Sandra.

"They ask him all these philosophy of life questions. They treat him like the Dalai Lama," Sandra told the *Los Angeles Times Magazine* in a 2000 cover story about her. "It really puzzles my sister and me how he always comes across as this folk hero. And we're going, he's not that, he's a total shyster. But the more you call him a shyster, the more people go, 'Oh, the angry daughters.'"

———

Loh and I spent another couple of hours looking at his photo albums and walking around the house. He betrayed a certain amount of pride in the fact that he and Alice dry all their laundry in the sun and have seven or eight large containers in the backyard to collect rainwater.

One of Loh's conversational refrains details the increasing frequency with which the human male needs to urinate as he ages. Toward the end of my visit, Loh told me that he had to "pee pee" and proceeded to walk into the backyard and relieve himself. I walked outside to bear witness.

"Well, you're saving a lot of water," I said supportively.

"Sometimes when I'm waiting for the bus I have to pee pee, so I do."

"You find a lawn or a bush and . . . ?"

"No, on the sidewalk."

"I see. You're an interesting man."

"One time a police saw me and gave me a ticket. But when I stood before the judge, the judge was an old man."

"So . . . what happened? What was the fine?"

"No fine. The judge sympathized."

———

SANDRA AND I met for dinner that night in North Hollywood. We gabbed and gabbed about life and work and her father. She told me how she'd noticed that he'd aged significantly in the past three years; he has, on occasion, lost consciousness in public, and paramedics have been called. "His ticker goes in and out," Sandra said. "But he has a resting pulse of forty-six. He has the constitution of a lizard." Sometimes acquaintances of Sandra's will track down her e-mail address through KPCC, and write her to say that they saw her father sleeping on a bench somewhere or stumbling along the side of the road. He's resisted all of his children's efforts to equip him with a medical-alert device, as he doesn't want the physical encumbrance.

In the thirteen years I've known her, Sandra has felt to me

like a sister but at the same time like a mentor or exemplar, because she is much more evolved as a writer than I am. If I've
always looked up to her—or west at her—as an example or for
guidance, I'd never done so more than now, having witnessed
her father's eccentric behavior and experienced what it might
feel like to be his child.

I was reminded here of the *Los Angeles Times Magazine* story,
which described the way Sandra's confusion and anger toward
her father had been balanced by a realization: "After my mom
died, I went through this feeling of Oh, my gosh, this is my only
parent I have left. This is my only link to the past, for better or
worse. No matter what friends you have, they're not going to re-
place your family. And the more you understand them, the more
you understand yourself."

But as Sandra and I talked, I could see that there was more
there, too.

"The older I get, the more sympathetic I get," Sandra told
me. "And the older I get, the more of his tendencies I see in myself. I love the value of a dollar more and more." She told me that,
when fund-raising for her two daughters' school, she is increasingly able to collar the other mothers in the parking lot—"I go
extreme immigrant." (My favorite Loh-family moment is from
1998. I'm sitting in Sandra's living room in Van Nuys with her
husband, Mike, waiting for Sandra and Loh and Alice to arrive;
Sandra is ferrying her father and stepmother to her house in her
car. Suddenly the phone rings: it's Sandra and company, pulling
into the driveway. Sandra announces, "We're here. The yellow
peril has arrived.")

I asked Sandra if her father's advanced age, too, hasn't entered into the equation here.

She said yes—"If you're over eighty and you get out of the
house on a regular basis, I respect you. He's eighty-seven. If he

wants to swim in the ocean or walk on the side of the road, let him."

She added, "I've released him to the universe."

———

I REJOINED LOH THE NEXT MORNING for swimming and exercises on the beach. Many of the themes we had established the day before were reasserted—he wore a backward sweater, and we ate dumpster bananas, and he peed on the lawn, and he turned off all the lights at the beach club, and he wore his preposterous Speedo, and he told me that he is able to drink ocean water even though it is dirty because he is "a dirty old man."

After we'd put our clothes back on in the changing room, he walked over to the sink and looked at himself in the mirror. Then he splashed some water on his head and patted down his mane, saying, "The hair—so people think I'm respectable."

When he looked over at me, he saw that I was laughing. So he laughed, too.

There were times during my quest that I ran into a force that I began to think of as Wisdom, Inc.

It started when I wrote an article about elder wisdom for *AARP* magazine—known fondly to most as *Modern Maturity* until a 2002 rebranding—and discovered that certain of the authorities and VIPs who'd turned me down for this book were willing to talk to me when I had a guaranteed audience of twenty-three million subscribers.

I got my second taste of Wisdom, Inc., when I went to hear the Dalai Lama speak at Radio City Music Hall one weekend. I entered the majestic Radio City to find His Holiness seated on a throne, surrounded by some eighty monks, all bathed in a gorgeous, end-of-day, mango-colored light. The Dalai Lama, by turns hilarious and profound, spoke about peace and meditation and suffering: "Cultivate an unbearableness toward others' suffering." At one point, he gazed into the audience and said, "Very nice hall, except the lights sometimes too strong" and donned a visor like you might see on an old-time cardsharp or bank clerk. I suppose I should have expected some non-traditional gestures from His Holiness—after all, he's the only Nobel Laureate to have appeared in an ad for Apple. When his Land Rover was

auctioned on eBay in 2007 (Sharon Stone announced the auc-
tion of the gas guzzler in a video on YouTube by saying, "You'll
just laugh the whole time that you're in it"), it fetched eighty
thousand dollars. But nevertheless I was surprised at Radio
City when, at speech's end, one of His Holiness's colleagues announced that it was time for the accountant's report. With that,
one of the monks stood and started rattling off the costs and
ticket-sales figures for the event. "Renting this extraordinary
theater, $648,846," he started, and then went on to cite figures
for staff costs, promotion, accommodations, et cetera.

But no encounter with the mercantile made a bigger impression on me than my relationship with a man I'll call Ted Bensen.
When I'd initially contacted Bensen, he'd asked me what I could
pay him for an interview, and I'd explained that journalistic ethics precluded my giving him money. Bensen seemed to understand. A few weeks later, he gave me a wonderfully funny and
perceptive interview, and we became fast friends. But then, a
few months later, he called and said he'd just had an experience
with another journalist that had left him feeling "used," and as
a result he didn't want me to publish my interview. I said, Let's
talk in a few months. When we did, Bensen hadn't changed
his mind. But then, when we talked in another few months' time,
Bensen said he might be willing to participate again—if I would
let him read the story before publishing it. I explained that I was
not allowed to do this, either. Bensen responded, "But if I did
your book, what would the compensation be?"

Something in my brain snapped here. Why, six months after
I'd told him that I was not allowed to pay him for an interview,
was I still having this conversation? I wanted to lash out, Mamet-
like, "*Fuck* the interview!" But I knew I might regret it. So I
pseudocalmly told Benson that we should both think about the
situation and then talk in a week or so.

I thought about it. And thought about it.

I'm not such a purist as to claim that wisdom must be wholly untouched by self-interest. Surely, almost all of the people I'd interviewed were motivated to some extent by a desire to bring attention to themselves or their books or their causes. And yet no one had actually boiled this self-interest down to a request for money. Which he then repeated.

I knew that I was going to have to tell Bensen that I couldn't use the interview, but I also knew that I wanted time to sulk and self-flagellate before telling him so. Bensen was hilarious and had a unique vantage point, and I would rue his absence. Why couldn't I just remove the two potentially troublesome parts of the interview and then read Bensen his quotes—or, in a pinch, let him read the whole piece and swear not to tell anyone I'd let him do so?

But I couldn't. I couldn't rationalize it or construct an argument that overruled my unease. My instincts wouldn't let me.

In the end, it came down to the word "discreet."

———

THERE WAS A FASCINATING EXPERIMENT done in 2000 by two academics, Masami Takahashi and Prashant Bordia, that speaks volumes about the difference between the conception of wisdom in Western and Eastern cultures. Takahashi and Bordia showed four groups of college students—one American, one Australian, one Indian, and one Japanese—all the possible pairings of the seven adjectives "wise," "aged," "awakened," "discreet," "experienced," "intuitive," and "knowledgeable." When the students were asked to rate which two adjectives were the most similar to each other, the Western students chose "wise" and "knowledgeable" or "wise" and "experienced," whereas the Easterners most associated "wise" with "discreet."

I called Takahashi, and he explained to me, "In the West, wisdom is more of an end product" and tends to be analytical, logical, and word-based. The Eastern conception of wisdom, though, is more like our idea of intuition and accords more value to qualities such as prudence and self-restraint. "In the East," Takahashi said, "wisdom is the search itself."

I asked Takahashi how he defined "discreet." He told me that, in the experiment, he and Bordia used the dictionary definition—exhibiting prudence and self-restraint.

This sort of helped me understand, but I realized that with Ted Bensen "discretion" had a more specific meaning. Discretion, I decided, is a kind of conduct. It's not wrong, of course, to want money or fame or respect or any number of other commodities—this is what, or is part of what, makes us individual. But if you're unable to pursue or make yourself available to these commodities while following the strictures of a given situation—strictures such as journalists not paying their subjects or letting them read stories before they're published—then your desires will outweigh your opportunities. You've lost your sense of proportion and context and have become the "plastics" guy in *The Graduate*. You are, in a word, unwise.

I called Bensen and told him I wouldn't be using the interview. I said that I felt that our postinterview conversations were "not in the right spirit of the book." He seemed to understand. We agreed to disagree. Our conversation had a strangely satisfying air of finality to it, rooted, I suppose, in our mutual unspoken realization that, despite all appearances to the contrary, we had not, in fact, wasted each other's time. Bensen now had a better bead on what not to say in interviews, and I had a stronger idea of what I thought wisdom was. And yes, I'd realized by then that I might make some use of the interview by not using Bensen's name, as I am doing right this second.

In the months since that last phone call, I've mentally thrashed over the relationship time and again. Sometimes I'll be reminded of something funny and slightly profane that Bensen said, and sometimes I'll wallow in my fear of having been high-handed or intransigent.

In my more visceral moments—in those moments directly after the third cup of morning coffee has brought me to an eye-watering, preorgasmic threshold—I often decide that Ted's and my friendship was like most of the memorable friendships in my life. Which is to say, we both got something from each other, but it was not the thing we thought we were going to get. This often seems the way—I thought that my friendship with an AIDS patient would fill me with a desire to live more fully and grandly, but instead it made me see the point of winnowing friends and interests down to the essential. I thought my friend who teaches college would make me want to read more classics, but instead he inspires me to travel and to buy expensive soap. You can't always predict what you'll get. And, in fact, getting anything at all is a blessing.

THERE IS, and always will be, opposition to the notion that older is wiser.

In 1945, Evelyn Waugh wrote, "Our wisdom, we prefer to think, is all of our own gathering, while, if truth be told, it is, most of it, the last coin of a legacy that dwindles with time."

Jack Meacham, a distinguished teaching professor emeritus at the State University of New York, wrote a 1990 essay, "The Loss of Wisdom," published in Robert J. Sternberg's collection *Wisdom: Its Nature, Origins, and Development*, in which he argued that older-is-wiser is a myth. Young people perpetuate the myth, Meacham wrote, because they want to believe that a gift awaits them, "else why continue to work hard and sacrifice?" And older folks perpetuate it because they want to believe that, in an ageist society in which they will lose their power, respect, and status, "there remain some special qualities that have been achieved in the course of life that cannot be stripped away by younger people." Meacham pointed out that the most oft-quoted incident of wisdom—the biblical King Solomon's decision to divide a baby in two in order to determine its real mother—happened when Solomon was young; yet "in old age, Solomon became rich and powerful and 'loved many strange women' who 'turned his heart after other gods' so that 'he kept not that which the Lord commanded.'"

Kathleen Woodward, a professor of English and the director of the Simpson Center for the Humanities at the University of Washington, has taken a different tack. Her point is not that older people aren't wise but rather that the celebration of older-is-wiser is often an impediment to social progress. In her 2003 essay "Against Wisdom: The Social Politics of Anger and Aging," she declared, "It is time to declare a moratorium on wisdom." Woodward argued, "Living up to the emotional (or unemotional) standard of wisdom can have the damaging consequence of suppressing the experience of appropriate anger." Certain progressive societal changes, such as the women's movement, would not have happened had they not been fueled by the rage of older people, she says. Claiming that wisdom justifies the disengagement theory of aging—the idea I mentioned earlier about how older folks withdraw from others so as to make their ultimate departure less disruptive—Woodward quotes both Gloria Steinem (who at age sixty wrote, "Age is supposed to create more serenity, calm, and detachment from the world, right? Well, I'm feeling just the reverse") and Germaine Greer (who, also at age sixty, wrote, "It's time to get angry again").

READING MEACHAM'S and Woodward's theories so close upon my dealings with Ted Bensen brought a lull to my quest. It wasn't that I didn't think older folks are wise, it was simply that it was so exhausting to separate the wisdom from the unwisdom. No one I'd met or read about exhibited 100 percent wisdom; wrongheadedness and the occasional act of lunacy seemed always to be intermingled with it. Granted, people like Granny D or Shirley Chisholm did not present a lot of discordant traits, but they were the exceptions. The more common paradigm was that presented by, say, Harold Bloom, who is brilliant but rarefied, if not elitist, or Eugene Loh, who is saving the world but peeing all over it as he does so.

Or look at the *I Ching*: for every lapidary bit of brilliance it offers, it also promotes utter loopiness like, "Deliver yourself from your great toe. Then the companion comes, and him you can trust." Or look at Socrates: some scholars accuse him—while he was gallivanting about, chatting up Athenians and ultimately deeming himself, but not them, wise—of abandoning his wife and family.

Somehow, rather than engaging me more fully, all of this contrary information had the effect of making me want to take a long nap. I needed something or someone to reanimate my sense of purpose. I needed, in short, to meet Ram Dass.

{ 18. }

I t comes down to your point of view.

In February 1997, Ram Dass, then sixty-five years old,
was lying in his bed in his Marin County home. He was trying
to think of a way to end *Still Here: Embracing Aging, Changing
and Dying*, the sequel to his 1971 *Be Here Now*, which helped
popularize Buddhist practices in America and which was once
the third-bestselling title in the English-speaking world, after
Dr. Spock's guide and the King James Bible. His editor had told
him that his new book seemed glib.

So Ram Dass—the former "neurotic Jewish overachiever"
named Richard Alpert who'd been fired from his professorship at
Harvard for giving out LSD to students with Timothy Leary and
then gone on to find inner peace in India, change his name, and
become a spiritual icon to millions—did an exercise. He tried to
imagine what it would feel like to be very old.

Just then, the phone rang. Standing to answer it, Ram Dass
suddenly collapsed on the floor when his leg gave out.

"That was probably the moment when I first stroked. When I
got stroked," he explains in the documentary *Fierce Grace*. Indeed,
Ram Dass later found out that he'd had a massive cerebral hemor-
rhage and that he'd had only a 10 percent chance of survival.

"I didn't have a spiritual thought—'I'm dying,' 'I'm going here'—no. None of these. All I remember is looking at the pipes on the ceiling," Ram Dass continues. "Here I am, Mr. Spiritual, and in my own death, I didn't, I didn't, I didn't . . . I didn't orient towards the spirit. It shows me I have some work to do."

In Ram Dass's case, the phrase "work to do" is not limited to his cast of mind: as a result of the stroke, he suffers from aphasia and is wheelchair bound, partially paralyzed, and dependent on round-the-clock care. He can't dress or feed himself or pee alone.

Originally he came to the somewhat startling conclusion that the stroke was a "gift" from his guru, the Maharajji—a viewpoint he changed when the Maharajji's successor wrote Ram Dass a strident letter saying that the Maharajji would never punish like that. Nevertheless, Ram Dass has emerged from his medical hell with a kind of optimism that inspires awe. He thinks the stroke is a *good* thing. √

Though this optimism was slow-growing, it was evident from the get-go that Ram Dass had not, poststroke, lost his sense of humor. A week after his ordeal, his doctor conducted a test of his patient's mental faculties. He held up a pen in front of Ram Dass and asked him its name. "A pen," Ram Dass said. The doctor pointed to a wristwatch and asked for its name. "Watch," the patient said. Then the doctor held his necktie in front of him for naming. Ram Dass said, "*Shmatte.*"

But Ram Dass's optimism is not merely confined to his sense of humor; it goes deeper. "I've grown to love my wheelchair (I call it my swan boat)," he writes in *Still Here;* pointing out that Chinese emperors and Indian maharajahs are carried on palanquins, he adds, "In other cultures, it's a symbol of honor and power to be carried and wheeled." Moreover, he finds that the silences that his aphasia bring to his conversation serve almost as a teaching tool—faced with the auditory void, his interlocutors tend to do that thing which most pleases a teacher: answer their own questions.

"I was galumphing through life before the stroke, and I kind of thought that was that," he sums up in *Fierce Grace*. "But the stroke is like a whole new incarnation. There are qualities that have come out that never would have."

———

ON THE PATH to enlightenment, we may encounter pebbles.

I'd flown to Maui.

Two days earlier, I'd sent Ram Dass an e-mail to reconfirm our appointment, and he had not written back, so I was starting to worry.

Walking along the ocean outside of a town called Paia one day, I fell into conversation with a scraggly, lived-in-looking gentleman of advanced age who was sitting on a stone wall on the edge of a beach. His frayed denim vest said "biker" or "world traveler" to me.

I found myself telling this man who Ram Dass is. "Basically his point is that a lot of our suffering is self-induced. He thinks we worry too much about the future and/or that we live too much in the past," I said, conscious of suddenly sounding very herbal tea, very spirituality seminar at the Knowledge Basement. "He thinks we should concentrate on the present."

"That sounds like a good thing," the beachcomber said, his greasy, long hair dully reflecting the harsh sunlight.

"It is," I corroborated. "But he also writes that 'in the present moment, there is no time,' so I'm, uh, a little worried about him keeping our appointment."

The man smiled and said, "Sounds like you're worrying too much about the future."

"I probably am. But I somewhat rashly spent $1,100 on a plane ticket, and I guess I'm finding it a little tough to Be Here Now."

"Yeah, if he's a no-show, that's definitely Was There Then."

I smiled bleakly. I stared at the blazing ocean, wishing it would magically cough up a slightly damp Ram Dass or an already transcribed interview.

It occurred to me: "Maybe I came all this way from New York because I was really meant to meet *you*, not him."

His face betraying no emotion, the man replied, "Could be, could be . . ."

"Do you have anything wise to tell me?" I asked.

"No."

"That doesn't really help me."

He shrugged his shoulders Yiddishly.

About six hours later, I ran into the man again as he and a female friend were leaving a funky-looking restaurant in town. The man looked slightly seasick. On seeing me, though, he brightened and called out, "Hey, Wisdom Guy!" He told his friend about how I had tried to plumb his mental depths earlier on the beach.

"So?" I asked him, mock-expectantly. "Any revelations or brainstorms since I saw you?"

"Yeah," he said, clutching his stomach and suddenly looking as wise as Solomon, "don't eat at this restaurant."

RAM DASS LIVES on the northern coast of Maui, about a quarter of a mile from the beach, in a large ranch house with a swimming pool and a big backyard. He still hadn't replied to my e-mail, but rather than calling him—I didn't want to harsh Mr. Spiritual's mellow—I'd simply showed up at the appointed time.

On approaching his front door, I added my sandals to a largish clump of six or seven other pairs: wisdom's ashtray. Some four minutes later, having passed through the living room—lots of incense and lots of colorful cloth wall hangings depicting knowledge-laden Asian men—and said good-bye to a documentary-film crew who had been filming Ram Dass, I found myself seated with him on the porch overlooking the pool.

Birds twittered. Ocean breezes wafted.

Ram Dass has a habit of craning his head slowly from side to side. This, combined with his fluffy white hair and beard, gives him the mien of a downy owl. Reaching for the tin of Swiss chocolates that the film crew had brought him, he handed it to me. I took it and said, "Oooh, chocolate."

"I'm not giving you the whole thing."

"OK."

I selected one and put the tin back on the arm of the wheelchair.

A silence settled over us. Ram Dass writes in *Still Here* that people use his silences as "a doorway to their inner quiet," but I knew that this was too soon in the conversation to approach that doorway, as the doorway was mostly filled with chocolate.

"How long have you been on Maui?" I asked.

"Two years. Why go anywhere else? I made a pact with myself never to fly anymore." He said that, as a lecturer—the profession he writes down whenever documents require him to specify his line of work—he'd gotten tired of being on planes. "It's made life easier for me. My brother died this week. My family would like me to be there for the deliberations, but I said to them, 'I'm not flying,' and that's hard for them. They don't understand it."

"But you'll go for the funeral, right?"

"No," he said. "I talk to my brother . . ."—and here he motioned up to heaven with his arm.

"Ah. I bet there are some angry e-mails and phone calls going around in your family."

"Yes," he said, with resignation.

———

RAM DASS THINKS that most of us, particularly when we get older, spend too much time dwelling in the past or worrying about the future, instead of existing as fully as possible in the present. He urges us to go from ego awareness (the state of mind in which we are prey to memories and passing anxieties) to soul awareness (a meditative state in which we are calm and unburdened).

To achieve this mindfulness, he suggests various kinds of meditation. One is "skygazing," an exercise found in the Tibetan Dzogchen practice: you lie down on your back and look up at the sky long enough that you start to think the sky is your own awareness and that the passing clouds are the phenomena that enter your mind and body—smells, sounds, fears, desires. "The sky doesn't pay attention to the clouds passing through. It just stays open as they all go by," he writes.

I'd tried this at the B and B where I was staying. Indeed, it had calmed me; but, like all meditation, it also made me feel light-headed and slightly numb. Less successful was my attempt to do a walking meditation—with your hands folded in front of or behind you, you concentrate on your breath and walk very, very slowly. This one, like all exercises in which I am told to be aware of my breathing, had the unfortunate result of reminding me of those acting classes where you are told to lie on a cold cement floor, push the small of your back against the floor, and *breeeeathe through your buttocks.*

Ram Dass's not going to his brother's funeral encapsulated for me both the greatest strength and the greatest weakness of his spiritual orientation. On the positive side, being able, in the face of death, to rely on one's own faculties and spiritual worldview was a powerful sign of one's own resilience and commitment to ideals. On the negative side, he wasn't going to his brother's funeral. It reminded me of a question I've always had about monks: is being a monk incredibly selfish or incredibly selfless? Moreover, I've always wondered about the practicality of purging oneself of one's demons—is it necessarily a good thing?

And so, on Ram Dass's porch, I found myself asking him, "How does mindfulness and soul awareness work vis-à-vis creativity? I find that as a writer what often gets pen to paper are the negative emotions—envy primarily, but also competitiveness and egomania."

He smiled wryly and said, "There's a doctor who said, 'I'm afraid that if I get too identified with my soul, I won't be a good doctor.'"

"Exactly."

"I said, 'You'll be a *better* doctor. You'll see the world in more levels of awareness. More levels of consciousness.'"

"So my envy will have new colors?"

"*Many* colors. You'll be able to witness the envy. But you won't be envious." Witnessing is the process by which one focuses intently on one's pain in an effort to defuse it; you try to know so much about it that you become smarter than it.

Anticipating my next question, Ram Dass continued, "Now, doesn't that hurt your writing? No. Your writing will be more joyful, and it won't be so negatively motivated, but it will still be motivated. Creativity comes from one place and one place only—intuition, or god inside. That's the only creativity. 'I'm creative' is bullshit."

"As an occasional pot smoker, I was interested to read that you think pot gives you soul awareness and that you think it's faster than meditation. So are we saying here that soul awareness has something to do with wanting to eat large bowls of Cocoa Puffs drenched in heavy cream?"

Long silence.

Finally he said, "I think that pot is a mild psychedelic. It gives you more flexibility in dealing with your consciousness. It's easier to shift from one plane to another—ego to soul—with pot." He explained that it's not the pot that takes one plane to plane, but, rather, it's one's own volition. We talked a little about LSD, which Ram Dass no longer uses, and he told me that Aldous Huxley's wife gave him LSD on his deathbed.

"Wow," I said. "That would be a beautiful way to go."

"There are a lot of beautiful ways to go."

"Tell me—given that you became enlightened at a young age, will you undergo less growth as an older person than most people will?"

"Well, first of all," he said, his heretofore beaming expression suddenly turning serious, "I'm not enlightened, so strike that."

"Well, you're *something*."

"Yeah, I'm something. My guru made me something. And what that something keeps me with is a very friendly attitude toward death, which means that I will not have fear during my old age."

Ram Dass writes in *Still Here* that our fear of death arises from the fact that we are philosophical materialists—that we believe only what we can see. He acknowledges that people of faith believe in an afterlife, but he asserts that this is largely speculative and has no direct influence on our earthly existence.

"But the fact that you received a lot of wisdom early on in life doesn't mean that you have less to grow?"

He stared at a point in space midway between my chin and my collarbone, and suddenly I saw what he meant when he said that people sometimes fill in his silences. I added, "Or is wisdom infinite?"

"Yes, it's infinite," he said, nodding his head and not needing to call me Grasshopper because the Grasshopper was implied. "Once you're in your wisdom, the time-space arc . . . My guru"—this is a dead person we're talking about—"can be in two places at one time. He could know what's going on in India from Boston. Because I've done my *sadhana*—my spiritual practice—I am less inclined to identify with my ego than I am with my soul. That means I relate to people differently. And I relate to death differently."

Ram Dass has helped create clinics for dying patients. He tells a story about an exercise that a nurse in a workshop he led once conducted. The woman had metastatic cancer. She asked everyone in the group what they would feel if they were visiting her if she was in the hospital after one of her surgeries. She wrote the group's answers on the board—pity, sadness, "I would be angry at God," et cetera. She concluded, "You see how lonely I was? Everyone was so busy reacting to my situation that nobody was there for me."

Ram Dass's clinics are an attempt to ameliorate this problem. Moreover, he is—insert your own LSD joke here—an advocate of self-medication for mothers in labor and for the dying. He cites studies showing that women given access to self-regulating pain medication during childbirth have used half as much as those who were medicated by hospital staff.

———

WE STARED AT THE OCEAN in the distance. Maui worked its gentle magic. The palms swaying sounded like the rustling of silk.

Ram Dass had been, despite the fact that one side of his body is paralyzed, fairly wiggly throughout our interview—he loves to gesture in big, swoopy arcs with his left hand; he moved himself around the porch by using both this arm and his left leg to make his wheelchair lurch forward. But in this quieter moment, his body was wholly at rest.

When the moment had passed, he looked over at me and asked, "Where in New York do you live?"

"In the West Village. Charles and Bleecker."

He broke out in a slightly sheepish smile and said, "I used to cruise that area."

This surprised me. Though, in more recent years, Ram Dass will sometimes mention his homosexuality during lectures, he doesn't write about it in his books, out of fear that it will limit his audience. I asked him if he was ever tempted or encouraged to downplay his drug use for the same reason, and he told me, "Well, partially my audience *comes from* my drugs. It doesn't come from my gayness."

But more than surprising me, the comment about cruising took me aback because it made me appreciate Ram Dass's struggle so much more than merely reading his books had. Somewhere in my mind, I lumped the cruising remark together with his earlier covetousness of the tin of chocolates and to his mentioning in *Still Here* how much he misses not driving his MG now that he's had a stroke. What emerged was a portrait of a man with great appetites. This suddenly made me appreciate his struggle over the years to attain mindfulness all that much more—it wasn't as if he were some breezy ascetic, untempted by the distracting, juicy plumpnesses of the world. He's a guy like you and me.

OUR CONVERSATION about homosexuality somehow morphed into one about fame. Ram Dass told me that he'd been friends with John Lennon, but when I excitedly asked follow-up questions about Lennon, Ram Dass grew vague and disinterested.

"I've had experiences in my life that take me beyond power and fame," he told me. "Most people want those two things. I don't want them."

"Did you ever?"

"Sure."

"When did it stop?"

"When I started to identify with my soul," he said. "I get invitations to go to famous things a lot because I'm an icon and I'm old."

"'Invite Ram Dass—he's famous *and he's old!*'"

"I say to them, 'I don't fly.' I—" He waved his hand good-bye.

"Has fame ever been a problem?"

"There was one time when it was. I was in Miami Beach once, and some women came up to me and started grabbing my buttons. They wanted the buttons off my clothes."

I suddenly realized that, of all the wise people I'd interviewed, Ram Dass was the only one whose fame had really entered into the equation for me. It had created expectations and hopes—I strongly wanted him to ask me to get high with him so I could tell all my friends that I had gotten high with the man who had not only gotten fired from Harvard for giving LSD to students, but who had later locked himself and five colleagues into a building for three weeks, during which they started to drink LSD straight out of the bottle. And when he'd offered me a glass of water early on, I fairly desperately wanted him to offer me a piece of fruit as well, because there is a tradition whereby, if a yogi offers you a piece of fruit, any wish you make will come true.

"What did you do?"

"I pushed them away. A lot of people like to be around famous people. It bores the shit out of me. I used to love famous people. My father did, too—he loved important people."

George Alpert had been the president of the New York, New Haven & Hartford Railroad and had helped to start Brandeis University.

Ram Dass continued, "But then I became one, and it's dross."

"It's not a very palpable affirmation of what you've done with your life?"

"No. It's nothin'."

I believed him when he said this—that is, I believed that *he* believed fame is nothin'—but I can't say I agree with him. Surely, a certain amount of adulation is, for many people, a reward or a goad or a boon. Movie star–caliber fame, of course, is often destructive, but it comes to such a limited percentage of the population that it seems luxurious to contemplate.

Right?

Or maybe I just don't understand. It occurs to me that there are some kinds of wisdom that I can't get a purchase on, perhaps because I am too callow to do so—as in the Jean Cocteau directive, "Whatever the public criticizes in you, cultivate. It is you." I once actually sat and wrote down all the criticisms that have come my way over the years, in an effort to understand what Cocteau was getting at. When I contemplated emphasizing all of them, I thought, This might be a fascinating exercise. Thirty seconds later I thought, Are you out of your fucking mind?

———

OF ALL THE OLD-TIMERS I talked to during my quest, none made a longer-lasting impression on me than Ram Dass. Other folks had elicited stronger emotional reactions from me (my stepfather, Setsuko Nishi, and a woman you're about to meet named Althea Washington). Others had provided more anecdotal fodder and thus had more frequently been the topic of subsequent conversations I had about my quest (Sylvia Miles, Eugene "Nice to have warm air there" Loh).

But no one got under my skin quite like Ram Dass had. Granted, he and the context of our interview were a stacked deck: he's a spiritual figure, but one whose countercultural cred makes him palatable to me. His fame or sway, and my acknowledgment of same, works to exaggerate my response to him. He lives in a spectacularly beautiful place that, in being the farthest from my home that I was to travel, required an outlay of time and funds that I might be anxious to justify. His (former) exuberant drug use makes my (current) far more limited use look not uncharming. He's funny. He's self-deprecating.

But in the end, it all came down to the stroke. I simply

couldn't let go of the resilience that he showed in the face of this particular adversity. It thrilled me. The image of him kicking his good leg out in front of him and then dragging his wheelchair forward is one I'll carry with me for a very long time.

I was moved, too, by the work that he has done with hospices and the dying. Shortly after I met Ram Dass, I interviewed Robert J. Sternberg, a psychologist and former president of the American Psychological Association who, in 1990, edited *Wisdom: Its Nature, Origins, and Development*, which I mentioned earlier. I called Sternberg at his office at Tufts University, where he's the dean of arts and sciences, to ask him how older people's wisdom is different from younger folks', and he told me about his Balance Theory of wisdom: "The way I define it is using your cognitive skills and your knowledge for the common good. So one way in which an older person has an advantage is that they have a better sense of what the common good is because they've been around longer to see the kinds of things that work and the ones that don't. Some things that might look good don't really when you look at them more closely. Common good is a very abstract concept, but it's something you learn from experience."

The second part of the Balance Theory is the balancing of interpersonal and extrapersonal goals: "In other words—your own interests, other people, and the larger truth. When you're younger, there's more of a tendency to get out of balance—you think, Well, I'm not going to care about my family because I really need to get that job or promotion. Or a mother may leave the workforce and then spend all her time with her kids, so that her career goes to hell. When you get older, you often begin to realize that you can't afford to say anymore, 'In five or ten years I'll balance my life.' When people say that, they often only say it and don't do it. You realize that your time is valuable."

The third component of the Balance Theory is balancing

long-term and short-term interests. "When you're twenty, you don't think about what's going to happen to you in forty years. When I look at some of the things I did when I was younger, it's sort of hard to believe I did them, they were so stupid. It's hard to have long-term perspective because you feel like the world is your oyster and everything is going so great. But by the time you're older and have lived through the school of hard knocks, you realize that you're going to pay the price. If you eat poorly or smoke or drink a lot, you come to realize that the long term is not an abstraction."

The fourth component of Sternberg's theory is dialogical thinking—the ability to understand other people's point of view: "As you get older, you're more exposed to different points of view, you see how different things play out. I tend to look at the Iraq war and think, haven't we been through this in Vietnam already? Your ability to see other points of view increases."

Sternberg has written that the difference between social intelligence and wisdom is that the former can be used for selfish ends. I brought this up and asked him, "If I bad-mouth a client or employer, they're not gonna hire me again. Isn't my knowing that a kind of wisdom?"

"For me, practical intelligence is about things that affect *me*," he said. "'I better act in a certain way so that I get hired or a promotion'—that's social intelligence. Wisdom is about things that have some kind of larger effect on common good. It affects you, other people, and institutions. Wisdom is more that if I act poorly toward other people, it sets a bad role model."

———

I LIKED THE ADDITION of common good to the definition of wisdom. After all, it's possible, I suppose, to bring healthy and appropriate amounts of doubt, nonattachment, and reciprocity into your life and still be, say, a bank robber. You doubt that some people should be rich while others are poor; you are nonattached to the consequences of your actions or to the law and thus are unfazed by the moral hazards of your crime; and perhaps you are so reciprocative as to share some of the stolen money with your accomplices and their families.

But a bank robbery is not for the common good. Therefore, common good is a valuable component in a definition of wisdom, and one that Ram Dass has practiced with gusto. If taking some of the sting out of the dying process is not a common good, then I don't know what is.

AFTER MY CONVERSATION with Charlotte Prozan in which I'd told her, "I like the ladies," I'd been thinking more and more about why I'm not usually warmed by old men. The amateur psychologist in me had lately, if rather obviously, dwelled on the fact that neither my father nor my stepfather were wholly able to resolve their substance-abuse problems. Part of me—and I'm thinking it's most especially the part that got kicked out of boarding school for smoking pot and that still enjoys a little after-dinner cannabinoid treat—doesn't want to be like either of them.

Old men come with their own set of problems. At least four people I talked to during my quest referred to old men as being sexually "used up." This fact, and the discrimination aimed at it, combined with many an older man's disinclination to form social networks, can, if he's white, render him a minority for the first time in his life. How he chooses to deal with this fact will color his dying days.

The Asperger's-like traits that are the hallmark of some men—social awkwardness and an inability to read cues—can intensify with age. A sixty-four-year-old Richard Nixon, three years after his 1974 resignation from the presidency, was interviewed by television host David Frost. Before one of the interviews, Nixon made a stab at establishing some male camaraderie by asking Frost, "Well, did you do any fornicating this weekend?" Frost later referred to the incident as "a mind-boggling moment. It was so touchingly clumsy."

I knew I wanted to look for theories or thoughts about the malaise of senior gents, and though I'd come across two fascinating ones, neither were specific to men. The first was Norman Mailer's assertion, during a 2007 talk the eighty-four-year-old gave at the New York Public Library, his final public appearance (not counting one via satellite), that "I really am a pessimist. I've always felt that fascism is a more natural governmental condition than democracy. Democracy is a grace. It's something essentially splendid because it's not at all routine or automatic. Fascism goes back to our infancy and childhood, where we were always told how to live. We were told, Yes, you may do this; no, you may not do that. So the secret of fascism is that it has this appeal to people whose later lives are not satisfactory."

The second was a passage from psychologist and *Soul's Code* author James Hillman's *The Force of Character*, in which he links old people's sagging posture and drooping body parts to their homing instinct to "the underworld beneath the grave, which can be entered long before the actual grave in the actual cemetery." Being an elder, Hillman writes, "calls for a learning about shadows, an instruction from the 'dead' (that is, from what has gone on before, become invisible, yet continues to vivify our lives with its influences)." Hillman writes, "This may account for some of the nastiness of old people, their thriving on wicked stories and twisted gossip, on surgical mistakes and bad doctors, crooked relatives, scandals, accidents, and ruined finances. They are tuned in to the underworld, so they go to sleep reading crime novels and watching cop flicks. They enjoy the vicious psychopathy of the heroes and heroines of afternoon soaps and the bizarre pathologies exhibited on talk shows."

But, again, neither Mailer nor Hillman was specifically addressing the subject of older men. I thought perhaps I was laboring under a highly personal view of this demographic subset until I decided to listen again to Mailer's "Live from the NYPL" lecture online. At one point, Mailer tells his interviewer, Andrew O'Hagan, that violence was the "last frontier available" to writers of Mailer's generation—nineteenth-century writers had already covered manners and love, and early-twentieth-century writers had already done sex. Mailer tells O'Hagan, "Violence had not been written about. I was drawn to it."

O'Hagan asks, "Was it during the writing of *The Naked and the Dead* or perhaps *An American Dream* that you realized your own personal capacity for violence?"

Mailer responds, "First of all, I think most men do. Most ✓ men suppress it. I certainly had suppressed it for many years. And then it began to come out. I began to feel that unless I came to terms with this violence—unless I learned some martial arts and to not be afraid of difficulties and street fights— that I would sicken within early. It was a deep inner feeling. I had to come to grips with violence. In the course of coming to grips with it, I became fascinated by it as well because I began to pursue the idea of how much morality there is in very violent people."

Mailer and O'Hagan continue talking for a while, and at one point Mailer confesses that he was upset that *The Naked and the Dead* was so successful because he realized no one would ever treat him as if he were anonymous again.

> Mailer: I wanted that because it enabled me to be an observer, and I loved that. It took me about twenty years to come to grips and make my peace with the idea that I was not going to have a life like most people, and I was probably not going to be able to write like most people.

O'Hagan: Or even most writers. You've had more celebrity probably than any other writer in America.

Mailer: It happened over and over. Then what happened, of course, was that moment in the early sixties when I stabbed my second wife. After that, there was no turning back.

O'Hagan: Norman, do you think that cost you the Nobel Prize?

Mailer: Well, I'll tell you one thing. Swedes are very intelligent people. And I think they'd be damned, they're damned, if they want to give their prize to a wife stabber. Sour and bitter as I could become, I don't think I could blame them. (*To audience:*) By the way, can you hear me in back?

(*Smattering of audience applause.*)

———

THE OTHER PERSON who helped me to understand the source of old men's grumbling was British comic novelist Kingsley Amis. From an article in *Bookforum,* I learned that Amis—a notoriously heavy drinker whose monthly whiskey bill in the late 1970s was one thousand pounds and who supplemented his more highbrow literary fare with three guides to drinks and drinking—contended that there were two kinds of hangovers. The first kind is the literal or physical kind, which we all know about. Amis is widely regarded as having written, in his 1954 campus comedy, *Lucky Jim,* the consummate description of a hangover:

> Dixon was alive again. Consciousness was upon him before he could get out of the way; not for him the slow, gracious wandering from the halls of sleep, but a summary, forcible ejection. He lay sprawled, too wicked to move, spewed up like a broken spider-crab on the tarry shingle of the morning. The light did him harm,

but not as much as looking at things did; he resolved, having done it once, never to move his eyeballs again. A dusty thudding in his head made the scene before him beat like a pulse. His mouth had been used as a latrine by some small creature of the night, and then as its mausoleum. During the night, too, he'd somehow been on a cross-country run and then been expertly beaten up by secret police. He felt bad.

The other kind of hangover is the metaphorical kind, and Amis felt that this kind was the particular province of old men. Intriguingly, however, Amis suggested that your ability to label this particular bit of old-man malaise specifically as "hangover" allows you to suck the poison out of the bite:

> When that ineffable compound of depression, sadness (these two are not the same), anxiety, self-hatred, sense of failure and fear for the future begins to steal over you, start telling yourself that what you have is a hangover. You are not sickening for anything, you have not suffered a minor brain lesion, you are not all that bad at your job, your family and friends are not leagued in a conspiracy of barely maintained silence about what a shit you are, you have not come at last to see life as it really is, and there is no use crying over spilt milk.

→ In other words, it depends on how you look at it.

For the past twenty years, my mother has been collecting sculptures and prints of cows. She has tin cows on metal spindles; she has tiny ceramic cows that graze coffee tables. She is cow mad.

I thought of her collection the day I drove into Croasdaile Village, her retirement community in Durham, surrounded as it is by meadows, pastures, a farmhouse, and, yes, cows. Buddha said that you are what you think; some people say that you are, or that you become, what you eat. But Mom's example suggests that you are what you dust.

I'd been at Croasdaile for only about five minutes when I was struck by the utter naïveté and wrongness of my earlier fear that Mom had moved to a retirement community in order to disengage. Mom had told me to meet her in Croasdaile's auditorium, where she was in rehearsals for a play she'd been cast in. We hugged hello, and she told me, "I've been asked to play Chiquita Banana!"

Apparently the role of the glamorous, singing, bolero-wearing banana-enchantress had been written into the play, a series of topical comic vignettes penned by another resident. When the director explained the new development, she said, "Only one person could play this part. Ann Earley."

I congratulated Mom. Clearly she was doing something right in her new life: her new friends thought she was capable of portraying fruit.

Mom introduced me to the director, saying, "This is my son, who's been associated with the theater," a locution that my brain somehow translated as "male whore."

Mom's one-bedroom apartment, in the main building, is at once cozy and spacious—wall-to-wall carpeting and lots of sunlight act as gentle tour guides to the apartment's four rooms and Mom's group of orchids. Once we'd settled ourselves in the living room, I asked Mom how she was doing, and she said she felt like she'd made the right decisions about leaving Will and coming to Durham. She said she's always loved trying to figure out a new situation and that Croasdaile had provided ample new information for her to parse. I asked if she'd encountered any stumbling blocks, and she said that the only one had been when one of her new friends at Croasdaile (which was founded by Methodists) asked her, "Have you accepted Jesus into your life, Ann?" Mom told me, "That's a language I don't speak." But she found that putting herself in her new life situation while she was still at the top of her mental game was unexpectedly flattering. "This is the Land of Unfinished Sentences," she told me. "Down here, I'm Mensa."

She said she was still talking to Will on a regular basis. "At first he'd call and try to get me to come back, but gradually he caught on," she said. As for her own emotional state vis-à-vis Will and the divorce, she said, "It's not a clear tear. It has a jagged edge."

Indeed, about an hour later, as we were walking down one of Croasdaile's many seemingly endless and brightly lit corridors, we found ourselves behind a couple in their nineties who were holding hands as they shuffled along. Mom looked at me and said, "I have a lot of little poignant moments where I see couples like that and think, 'You bitch, you could be pushing Will's wheelchair.'"

———

You haven't told me what you think about the divorce," Mom said, overturning a huge cardboard box onto the floor of her bedroom. The box contained Mom's project for me during my stay: a cast-iron bench in the shape of a butterfly with outspread wings, which she wanted me to assemble. An hour earlier, Mom had shown me a photograph of the completed bench. "It's going to be *darling*," she'd said. Then she acknowledged, "This is the kind of furniture you could *never* have with a man in the house."

We knelt on the floor and started pulling the wings and the seat out of the box. That I was constructing a cast-iron butterfly in my newly divorced mother's apartment was not lost on me; I characterized the bench as "a giant literary symbol." Mom grimace-smiled, and I knew this was my cue to answer her question about the divorce.

I'd been thinking a lot about it and had come to the conclusion that Mom's decision was not scam-based. Greg had recently been in a three-day-long funk, and by the end of the three days I'd longed to scream, "New mood, please!" But Will's funk has lasted years. Of *course* you'd get yourself away from that, I'd decided—anyone would.

"It's been really hard to see you guys in so much pain," I offered up as I wrangled one of the large, heavy wings into upright position and leaned it against the wall. "But I think you've made the right decision."

"Do you think of Will as your father?" she asked.

"Not really," I said. I'd started going away to school shortly into Mom and Will's relationship.

"The second wave of my reaction," I continued, "was the

more selfish one that one has in the presence of breakups. It's really hard to watch two people split up and not think about your own relationship—and not think, There but for the grace of God."

"Right."

We'd pulled the four pieces of the literary symbol out of the box—two wings, a body, and the bench's seat.

"But in the end," I said, "I worry more about Will than about you, right? I mean, divorce is always harder on men because they don't have the social networks and support that women do."

Mom said I was probably right.

I spent the next hour and fifteen minutes trying to assemble the literary symbol. The pieces of the metal, though no longer than three feet in any one direction, were hefty and difficult to manipulate. They were to be connected by bolts, but the bolts were unwilling to conform to the dictates of the tools that Mom had supplied me. When I'd finally managed to get the three main pieces of the bench fastened to one another, we realized that I had two of the pieces backwards and needed to start over.

"This is really hard," I said to Mom. "And it's moments like this that being gay really doesn't help me."

"I know," Mom clucked. "The furniture that no man would live with is furniture that only a man can build."

———

KENDY LIVES ABOUT FIFTEEN MINUTES from Croasdaile. She came over the next day to lead a water-aerobics class in Croasdaile's indoor pool. Mom and I suited up and joined Kendy and eight Croasdaile residents—all women. Twisting and bending and gliding through the water, I was surprised by what a good work-out this was. I admired these women for making their efforts.

But my admiration was doubled the next day when Kendy took me to her water-aerobics class at the recreation center on the other side of town. The three people who showed up for this class were all older black women, none of whom could swim.

"Pools were segregated when I was young," one of the women told me. "We'd go to the swimming hole sometimes, but we'd always get a whuppin' with a switch for that."

I noticed that these women, not unsurprisingly, held on to their noodles—long, pliable flotation rods—more aggressively than the Croasdaile women had. One of them, a retired academic, told me, "I said to myself, as soon as I retire, I'm going to learn how to swim."

"And isn't it kind of terrifying?" I asked, thinking first of traumatic swimming lessons I'd had in childhood and then of the fact that, although I swim twice a week, I swim almost exclusively the breaststroke because I don't like to hold my head under the water.

She told me, "No, I can swim. I just can't swim and breathe."

A few minutes later, I floated out toward the four-foot waterline, where I fell into conversation with another of the women.

"This isn't scary for you?" I asked.

"No, I'm good," she said. "But I have my comfort zone."

The calm way she rotated her body in order to face me betrayed her excellent noodle management.

"And what *is* your comfort zone?" I asked.

"We're in it."

———

THAT AFTERNOON, Mom and Kendy and I drove to a nearby mall to look for a Chiquita Banana costume. The other cast members would be singing the Chiquita Banana song, during which Mom, dressed in an unspecified manner, would have about ninety seconds to engage in unspecified activity. Early on, one of the cast members had suggested Mom simply peel and eat a banana for ninety seconds, but Mom's immediate response to the suggestion—"Oh: oral sex"—bespoke an essential resistance to the idea. Subsequently, Kendy had found a shimmy-based Chiquita Banana dance routine on YouTube that Mom liked; the three of us had stood in front of Kendy's computer, gyrating and aping the routine along to the video, and I had thought, Oh my God, my life has turned into a Diane Keaton movie.

So Mom knew that she wanted to shimmy, but she didn't know what she wanted to wear while doing so.

"And do you see yourself holding a real banana, or a papier-mâché one?" I asked Mom.

"I don't want to use real fruit because I'll crush it."

"Crush it? How powerful is your shimmy?" I asked. "That's a shimmy from another dimension."

Once at the mall, we found a Party City store. Forty-nine dollars later, Mom was the proud owner of a florid yellow banana costume. As we waited in line at the cash register, Mom excitedly told me, "This could be a whole new beginning for me."

I thought, As . . . a piece of fruit?

On my fourth and last day in Durham, Kendy and Mom and I had lunch in the Croasdaile dining room. Mom seemed slightly pressed for time—she had a 1:30 bridge game, but 1:30 really meant 1:15, because there was always a mad rush for tables, and certain of Mom's colleagues—the "macular degenerates"—liked to sit at a particular shady table.

As we lunched, Kendy told us that the last time she'd talked to Will, he'd asked if he was still invited to Full Frame, which would happen again six months hence and at which we'd be celebrating Mom's eightieth birthday this year. Kendy, uncertain how to respond, had awkwardly said sure.

"He won't be around by then," Mom said. "All that lying in bed and smoking cigarettes. I don't think he has that long left."

At one point during the lunch, Kendy asked Mom, "What's going on with your eyelid?" Mom's right eyelid did look slightly droopy.

"My eyelids are starting to fall," Mom explained. "And when they do—"

"We'll put a lily in your hand," Kendy said.

———

KENDY DROVE ME to the airport.

"That lunch was the only time it got sad for me," I said. "Sitting in the dining room amidst all those scooters and walkers. At one point I looked across the room, and it was only women diners."

"It can be hard," Kendy said.

"Yeah."

"And at a certain point it'll get hard with Mom, too."

"I know. And it goes without saying, of course, that you're not in this alone."

"Of course, of course. I realize that."

"Any time you want one of us to step in, or you want to take a break . . ."

"Thank you. I'll keep you posted."

Kendy sent an e-mail a couple of weeks later to say that though the play at Croasdaile "didn't reach the level of expertise of *Waiting for Guffman,*" it went fairly smoothly—"People forgot fewer lines the night of the show as compared to the dress rehearsal." More important, Mom's turn as Chiquita was a hit—"It just made you want to run out and get a banana."

———

I TALKED TO KENDY a couple months later, and she told me how much she was loving having Mom be more of a presence in her life. They'd found the perfect balance of being together and being apart—they would chitchat and gossip for ten or fifteen minutes every Tuesday and Thursday, just before Kendy taught water aerobics at Croasdaile; very occasionally they would go on movie or lunch dates. I was reminded of a conversation I'd once overheard between Mom and a friend of hers. The friend had begun, "Ann, we see each other so infrequently," and Mom had completed the thought with "which is probably why we like each other so much."

We discussed Will, whom Kendy had just had a phone call with. His mood had been dark. Kendy told me, "Part of me wants to get up there and visit him. But you drop in, you get a snapshot of his life—what does it help?"

"Exactly. A lot of people have reached out to him, but I think he wants to be alone."

"For a long time he was calling Mom and asking her if she was ready to come home, but he's stopped that."

"Good," I said.

I asked if he'd mentioned Full Frame and Mom's eightieth again.

"Yeah. It came up. This time he said, 'I'm not sure I can make it.'"

———

IT USED TO BE, when I thought of my old age, that I tended to cling to two paradigms. One was the *Golden Girls* one, wherein three friends and I (they would be younger than me, because I'm the potty-mouthed nonagenarian in this fantasy) live together in a warm climate. We have a lanai, and in our backyard we grow one of the luxury fruits, possibly raspberries or figs. Copious amounts of Scrabble are played. We achieve local notoriety for our mai tais made with rubbing alcohol. At our annual Christmas party, someone has sex in a wheelchair. When the blender starts whirring at sundown, everyone slips into muumuus.

The other paradigm is one I've been incubating for a long time and is derived from an account I read of an aged English acting legend. Apparently she and her husband had shown up at the matinee of a play in the West End just as the curtain was rising. Noisily and distractingly making their way through the audience—they were both carrying satchels, wet umbrellas, and bags "full of shopping"—the pair finally settled into their seats some six minutes into the first act. At which point the woman turned to her husband and announced, "I *do* love a play, don't you?" (This paradigm is particularly appealing to me, I realize, because it doesn't require me to take any action beyond what I'm doing at the present; I already am this person.)

But now Mom had established a new paradigm for me. Her setup—enroll in summer camp but have a relative or friend nearby who occasionally gets you away from it—strikes me as possibly preferable. Moreover, it would still allow for the more essential elements of the previous two paradigms (potty mouth, figs, Scrabble, matinees, bags of shopping).

I hope you'll come visit.

{ 20. }

I threw my back out. This happened, ironically, while I was swimming—the very activity that most doctors recommend for people who have thrown their backs out.

For a period of two weeks, my upper torso was canted at a thirty-five-degree angle. I walked at one third of my normal speed. The pain was, on the whole, not great, but getting up from a seated position was difficult and sometimes elaborate. The only time the pain was harrowing was if I twisted suddenly or if I sneezed; both these activities sent shivers up my torso.

My most prevalent symptom was a slight irritableness. Certain standing positions were uncomfortable. So if this discomfort struck me when I was standing in line at the drugstore—as it did one day—then I found myself peevish with slow-moving salesclerks. I didn't actually say anything to the heavyset clerk in his twenties at the drugstore near my office, but believe me, he felt my scorn.

That it now took me half an hour instead of ten minutes to walk from my house to my office was not a big deal. Nor was it bothersome to me to run into friends or colleagues, four of whom saw fit to liken me to "an old man." But what *was* hard for me—or more specifically, hard for my ego—were those times when I ran into, or was about to run into, guys I flirt with in our neighborhood. Nothing has ever happened with these gents— I'm a happily coupled spouse—and I'm pretty sure nothing ever will, which seems to be the point of these little pools of charm. These are simply handsome men who live in my neighborhood, some of whom I've only ever said "Hello" to and with whom I've been sharing knowing smiles on the sidewalk for years. They are like mirrors, allowing me to gauge my ego's worth. I tried my best to avoid these men during the first week of my old-man-hood—one time I ducked behind a corner, twice I walked several blocks out of my way—because I didn't like the idea that I had lost my appeal.

But by the second week of my injury, I realized that I couldn't keep avoiding these guys and that it was silly and vain to do so. So, knowing that I was going to be walking past the store in which one of them works, I worked up a deflection scheme: I would, immediately upon contact, introduce a topic so juicy and interesting that my hunched-over posture and slight irritableness would go unnoticed.

And so I found myself outside a certain Bleecker Street emporium, being waved at by one of these men. When he motioned me to enter the store, I did and blurted, "I just saw a flying manhole cover!"

The flying manhole cover is the El Dorado of the urban pedestrian. I spent twenty-six years in New York City hearing about them and reading about them without seeing one. What usually happens is that the insulation on the copper electrical wiring that's underground cracks, or is burned by excessive demand, releasing carbon monoxide, which builds up and can be ignited by a spark, causing the manhole covers embedded in the street to burst and fly with a terrifying and dangerous vigor up into the air. Some of these three-hundred-pound cast-iron jobbies have flown as far as fifty feet.

I hadn't *just* seen the manhole cover—it had happened the day before—but it felt like it had just happened. The slight fudging of the where and when seemed to be superseded by my newly minted conviction that the distribution of interesting but slightly weird information is a necessary good and one that more people should engage in. We were not put on this planet to bore one another—there's televised fishing for that.

My deflection technique did its dirty trick. All attention was shifted from my physical state by the verbal torrent I was offering.

I'd like to think that, as I age, my ego will need less and less affirmation, but such a mind-set is probably naïve. My looks will fade, my power will wane, my money will be spent or diminished by rampant inflation, my wit will grow softer, my hipness will grow stale. But I will still have my mind. This gives me a great feeling of security; it's like knowing that even once you run out of sea-soaked saltines, you can still eat the boat. I simply need to get in the habit now of compensating for my ultimate wanings.

I'm going to have to see a lot more exploding manholes.

"Are you still enjoying spending so much time with members of my generation?" Mom asked me over the phone one day.

"I am, but . . ."

"But what?"

"But I've never met a group who's in such a goddamn rush all the time."

I explained that Granny D had chastised me for being five minutes late for our interview and that two other people I'd interviewed had mentioned the tick-tick-ticking of the clock. I'd also just read in *Time* a rare interview with Cormac McCarthy—in his seventy-four years, this was the third he'd ever given—that was conducted by Joel and Ethan Coen in celebration of their film adaptation of McCarthy's novel *No Country for Old Men*. At one point, Ethan Coen asks McCarthy if he ever has to curb an impulse toward outrageousness when he's writing, and McCarthy responds, "No, not really. Because I think that's misdirected . . . There's lots of stuff that you would like to do, you know. As your future gets shorter, you have to . . ."

"Prioritize?" Joel Coen asks.

"Yeah. Somewhat," McCarthy answers. "A friend of mine,

who's slightly older than me, told me, 'I don't even buy green bananas anymore.' I'm not quite there yet, but I understood what he was saying."

Before I started spending a lot of time with older folks, I thought that their occasional impatience and inflexibility was an outpouring of their bodily aches and pains, or it was a world-weariness they had accumulated over the years, or it was whatever psychological state is produced when a sense of entitlement is married to a gastric malady. It hadn't occurred to me that they were rushing to finish up.

I wish I'd had this perspective when I'd gone to interview Edward Albee.

———

In recent years, Edward Albee has included an instruction to nearly every line of dialogue in his plays. For instance, in *Occupant*, his 2002 play about the sculptor Louise Nevelson, ten of the first act's last fourteen lines have instruction attached to them—"Impressed," "Pause," "Sudden thought," "Noncommittal," "Genuine; slow," "Sudden awareness," "Preoccupied," "Genuine smile," "Quite disturbed," "Starting to exit." When the reader reaches the bottom of this page of the script and sees "CURTAIN," he's almost surprised by the absence of "With feeling."

I thought about these directives the day I went to talk to their seventy-nine-year-old author.

I'd walked to the TriBeCa address that Albee's assistant had given me, rung the doorbell, heard a lot of static, waited about two minutes, and then rung again. Appearing abruptly about fifteen feet away from me on the other side of the loading dock I was standing on, the mustachioed and handsome Albee—trim, with a prominent chest, and wearing a beige linen shirt and tight-fitting jeans—asked, "Did you ring a second time?"

"Yes."

"I said I'd be down. You didn't hear me?"

"No, I didn't," I said, having heard only the barrage of static. "I'm sorry." I nervously added, "The traffic is really loud here."

"That's OK."

Was it? His expression did not convince me.

After a more-than-usually awkward ride up a freight elevator, we entered his huge, airy loft. Seeing lots of tribal masks and sculpture, I enthused, "It's like going to Africa in here."

"Or many other countries," Albee corrected me.

He motioned for me to sit, and I reminded him that I was writing a book about wisdom.

"Define it," he said, hunkering down into one of the loft's chocolate-brown leather couches. "I forgot to look it up in the dictionary. What does it mean?"

"I have my own definition," I said, also sitting.

"You better know what the dictionary definition is."

"I have seen it," I lied, eager, now that we had established that I was deaf, not to add "unprepared" to my portfolio of liabilities. "I've not memorized it."

"What does it have to do with?" he asked.

"It has to do with universal knowledge," I vamped.

"What's 'universal'?"

"The way I'm defining it is, things which are understandable to nonspecialists."

"Define nonspecialists," he said.

I flashed him a look that I hoped translated as "*Helllllp.*"

He continued, "Sorry—I have to know what we're talking about."

I'D BEEN FOREWARNED of Albee's exacting nature. In a 2002 *New Yorker* profile of Daryl Roth, one of the producers and backers of Albee's *The Goat: or, Who Is Sylvia?* Albee had gone so far as to correct Roth on the pronounciation of his name. (It's AWL-bee, not AL-bee.) I'd also read up on Albee's difficult past and wondered if the messiness thereof didn't somehow fuel the great efforts he seems to take to keep his present orderly and precise.

Albee was rejected by his first family and then rejected his second. Born in 1928, he was abandoned by his birth parents as an infant and then adopted by the wealthy heirs of the Albee vaudeville houses family, who offered pampering but not love. Due to his habit of not attending classes, Albee had a checkered academic career but managed to graduate from the boarding school Choate; he was expelled from Trinity College after a year and a half. Shortly thereafter, he had a huge fight with his parents—he'd come home late one night and left the car covered in vomit—that resulted in his getting into a taxi and never returning. He didn't go to his father's funeral, and he didn't see his mother for another seventeen years. A decade later, after having written a lot of poetry, he burst onto the theatrical scene with *The Zoo Story* in 1958 and achieved greater renown with *Who's Afraid of Virginia Woolf?* in 1962. Though Pulitzer Prizes were to be awarded him for *A Delicate Balance* in 1967 and *Seascape* in 1975, he underwent a fifteen-year period of being persona non grata on Broadway. He broke the spell in 1994 with *Three Tall Women,* a searing, autobiographical look at his adoptive mother, for which he received his third Pulitzer, and followed it with 2000's *The Goat,* about a husband who has an affair with a goat.

Albee told me that he thinks wisdom is a matter of perspective. He said, "Maybe it's finally being able to figure out what you should be worrying about and what you shouldn't be worrying about."

"William James said that wisdom is knowing what to overlook."

"People worry about things and can't go to sleep at night because they're thinking about something they have to take care of the next morning at ten. That's rather silly, isn't it? If you just go to sleep, you can worry about it the next morning and take care of it. Because most important is to be able to participate as fully as possible."

Because it is one of the overarching themes of the Albee canon, I wanted to talk with him about how our lives are defined by the inevitability of death. In *The Zoo Story*, later expanded into *Peter and Jerry*, a meeting of two men in a park becomes suddenly traumatic when one of them impales himself on a knife he puts in the other's hand. In *Who's Afraid of Virginia Woolf?* George, who may have killed his parents, "kills" the son that he and Martha pretend to have. In *Three Tall Women*, a ninety-two-year-old woman who's had a severe stroke interacts with two of her younger selves.

"It's been suggested that maybe *Three Tall Women* gains some of its power from your having accepted death," I said.

"I accepted death when I was fifteen," he said animatedly. Off in the distance I could hear the low-pitched flatulence of a steam shovel or tractor. "As soon as I started reading. The only two things to write about are life and death. I disapprove of death. I don't want anything to do with it. I think it's a terrible waste of time."

"One of the characters in *Three Tall Women* says that children should be made aware they're dying from the moment they're born. Do you believe that?"

"Oh, yes, certainly. I think the awareness of the tentativeness of everything and the termination of everything should be enough to keep you mentally agile and interested. Accomplishing as much consciousness as you possibly can for the futile end of its all going away, that paradox being important. So people who turn off from participating in life—they're cushioning themselves for an awful kind of gesturing life, it seems to me. I've known people who stop participating as soon as they're forty. Mostly Republicans, of course. I'm always puzzled by people whose social and political values change as they get older—people who get more conservative. The desire to accumulate comfort and wealth—that's a deadening."

"Why do you think it happens to them?"

"They get scared, I suppose. Nobody wants to go away. Well, I know some people who are quite ill who want to go away," he said, sighing. "That's the one bad thing about getting to a certain age: your address book."

———

In the 1960s and 1970s, Albee had a reputation for being a bit of a mean drunk—he was sour and abusive to dinner-party companions; he once walked out of a play midact, hurling insults at the cast. He stopped drinking and smoking with the support of Jonathan Thomas, a painter and sculptor he met in 1971 at the University of Toronto; Albee and Thomas were together until Thomas's death of cancer in 2005.

I asked Albee, "How did stopping drinking change you?"

"It made me realize that the majority of my friends were nowhere near as amusing as I used to think they were."

"The veil was lifted?"

"Oh, boy. It's the same thing that happens when you get hearing aids," he explained. I'd not noticed until now the beige piece of plastic in his right ear. He continued, "Everyone has a certain amount they should drink in their lives. Some people do it throughout their lives, and some of us concentrate it in a five- or ten-year period."

"John Gielgud once called you a 'surly pirate with a drooping mustache,' and Philip Roth criticized your 'ghastly pansy rhetoric.' Is there a connection between people saying corrosive things about you and the fact that you've been a corrosive person yourself at times?"

"I'm always surprised when people who don't know me attack my work. It's always more virulent than the subject would permit. All the attacks seem infinitely more personal than they are with other writers. Which is curious. I do shoot my mouth off about things that I think are wrong—and I think one should. ✓ But you pay a price for that. I was never surly with John. I was shy, of course. Sometimes that can appear to be surly. The Philip Roth thing was inexcusable."

Given that we were plumbing the darker depths of Albee's career, I thought it might be an opportune time to ask about the period in which he fell out of favor on Broadway. I said, "There was this fifteen-year period or so in which—"

"I was out of fashion," he said, anticipating my question. "It all began when I made the mistake of writing *Who's Afraid of Virginia Woolf?* Not that I'm unhappy I wrote it—it's one's old-age pension. But everybody expected me to write that play over and over again. *Son of Who's Afraid of Virginia Woolf. Virginia Woolf II, III,* and *IV.* They wanted that. And what did I give them next? *Tiny Alice,* a metaphysical melodrama. That upset them. I didn't go back to write that kind of naturalistic play for a long time. I was making experiments. Also at that time I was getting really fed up with the state of criticism—theater criticism and all arts criticism. And I was making the mistake of shooting my mouth off about it. And critics have long memories."

I asked him if this had been a difficult period in his life.

"Well, I was having productions in Europe and around the country. Productions in New York. Just not on Broadway. It was annoying. But I was teaching, writing, going about my business, so it didn't bother me. You don't let the fuckers get ✓ you down."

"Most writers have a good twenty or so years in them, but you've had more like forty," I said.

"It's close to fifty."

But, really, who's counting?

———

GIVEN THE THEME of impending death that lurks in so many of Albee's plays, I asked him if he spent many of his waking hours contemplating his own demise. He said he did not. "And I never thought about being old until my lover Jonathan died. He and I were together thirty-five years. He died two years ago. All of a sudden I found myself bereft."

"I'm sorry."

"No, I'm recovering from it. If you're not willing to have loss, then you can't have gain. Thirty-five great years, and then he got cancer. It's been a rough time. But you go on."

A few months later, Albee told a reporter from the *New York Post*, "I learned something important about dying, about a slow death, as Jonathan's was. What I learned was: Never forget who's dying. It's not about you. It's always about them. And I learned something about grief: It never ends. It's like a third arm."

———

THERE ARE TWO PIECES OF WISDOM that I find in Albee. One is that love and hatred coexist in most alliances. He's a master of chilling depictions of tough love. In *The Goat*, the wife's rage, on learning about her husband's love affair with a four-legged creature, reaches a peak of vengeful fury that is astonishing. In the Broadway production with Mercedes Ruehl and Bill Pullman, the wife's final entrance—I don't want to give away too much here—caused my jaw literally to drop and to remain agape for fifteen seconds.

In the more abstract and mysterious *The Play about the Baby*, which was performed Off-Broadway in 2001, an older couple take an intense interest in a young couple's newborn. When the baby disappears, the older couple—who are death? The future? Older versions of the young couple?—psychologically terrorize the new parents into denying the existence of the baby. The older man even goes so far as to throw up into the air a bundle of blankets that looks to be the baby but is not, causing the young father to say, "You have decided to hurt us beyond salvation." But, as it turns out, the older couple are operating under the assumption that they are *helping* the other couple. The older man explains his and his partner's perverse mandate. "Wounds, children, wounds. If you have no wounds, how can you know you're alive?"

You could say that the theme of fierce ambivalence in human relations has been present in Albee's work for a long time. After all, late in *Who's Afraid of Virginia Woolf?* he has Martha explaining how George is her one true love: "George who is good to me, and whom I revile; who understands me, and whom I push off; who can make me laugh, and I choke it back in my throat; who can hold me, at night, so that it's warm, and whom I will bite so there's blood; who keeps learning the games we play as quickly as I can change the rules; who can make me happy and I do not wish to be happy, and yes I do wish to be happy. George and Martha: sad, sad, sad." But I would argue that Albee has, in his more recent works, brought the theme to its full fruition. More than ever, he shows how, even in some of the best unions, there are always traces of incompatibility. The bluebirds are forever speckled with black. Albee's prognosis vis-à-vis this duality of emotion is usually bleak. But sometimes he seems to be saying, in classic "What doesn't kill you makes you stronger" fashion, that the points of dissension within a union, if survived, may serve to make that union stronger.

The other piece of wisdom runs through both Albee's life and work and can be distilled to the words "pay attention." Albee's eagle eye has helped him a couple of crucial times during his career—such as when, as a young man, he visited a gay bar in Greenwich Village and saw, scrawled in soap on a mirror, a graffito that years later was very important to him. ("Who's afraid of Virginia Woolf?") Or the time in 1953 that the young aspiring poet Albee showed Thornton Wilder some of his poems. They were sitting by a lake in New Hampshire, drinking bourbon and lake water. Wilder placed one of the poems on the surface of the water and watched it float away as he asked Albee, "Have you ever thought about writing plays?" Apparently, Albee took note.

But I don't mean "pay attention" in a purely literal sense. Sometime in the mid-1990s, Albee filled out a questionnaire that a teacher on Long Island had sent him. When asked what had been the happiest time of his life, Albee responded, "Now. Always." He explained, "That's the only way to avoid regret, isn't it? If one loses one's talent, if one's ill and poor and lonely, if something that hideous were to happen to me, I would hope that I would still find something interesting about the experience."

As it turns out, Albee's most personal play, *Three Tall Women*, ends with the three women talking about when each of them was, or will be, happiest. The youngest says that she feels silly looking back and then expresses her hope that her best days are yet to come. The oldest—now on her deathbed—says you're happiest "When it's all done. When we stop. When we can stop."

But it's the middle woman who Albee has claimed in interviews is the wise one of the three because she has given up her illusions and is able to see into the past and the future. Or, as she explains in the play, "Enough shit gone through to have a sense of the shit that's ahead, but way past sitting and *playing* in it."

Like her creator, she says her best time is "now; now . . . always."

———

A COUPLE OF MONTHS after I'd talked with Albee, Greg and I went downtown to Pace University one night to hear him introduce a screening of *Who's Afraid of Virginia Woolf?*

Albee told the audience of three hundred or so people that Hollywood mogul Jack Warner had bought the play for Bette Davis and James Mason. Albee thought this a grand idea, especially as, early on in the play, Martha does a Bette Davis impersonation ("What a dump!"), so Davis would be doing Davis.

But, of course, through the vagaries of Hollywood filmmaking, Bette Davis and James Mason turned into Elizabeth Taylor and Richard Burton, and a screenplay that consists almost entirely of Albee's dialogue yielded a screen credit "Screenplay by Ernest Lehman." Lehman was the producer who hired himself as screenwriter and who, in one draft, had the ignorance and gall to make George and Martha's imaginary son a real, living son who is deeply retarded and living in the attic. (The *Mad* magazine parody of the movie also featured a living son.)

The movie version "opens out" the play by having the two drunken couples take a trip to a roadhouse. Albee told us, in what seemed only slight exaggeration, "With the exception of two sentences, every line of dialogue is mine. Here's the first sentence I did not write: 'Let's go to the roadhouse!' The second sentence I did not write goes something like, 'Hey, let's come back from the roadhouse!'"

Albee told us that he considers the finished film "pretty good," particularly when he considers what it *might* have been—"They had the rights, they could have turned it into a swimming picture."

But his problems with the movie are the excessive use of music, which he thinks forced the audience to feel certain ways and about which he said, "I learned a lot from that. I learned not to let people put music in your play." He added, "One of the things you learn as a playwright is that you own the play. They can't fuck around with it."

Even sitting fifty yards away from Albee in the large auditorium, I could sense his years-long irritation with the movie-making process. Control had been wrested from him. Precision was no longer his. No statement he made that evening betrayed this sentiment more than this one: "The film is black-and-white. But I had written the play in color." ✧

{ 22. }

Ir it took me an unconscionably long time to get down to visit Mom at Croasdaile, it took me downright forever to call Will and see how he was bearing up.

The Alfords—including Mom and Kendy and her husband, Rick, who all drove up from Durham—had spent a lovely Thanksgiving at Fred and Jocelyn's house near Hartford. But Mom had been anxious about Will throughout the festivities, as he had fallen down a week earlier. Mom had called him three days earlier, and he hadn't called back.

"He's my phantom limb," she told us. "So I worry."

The day after Thanksgiving, as we were all sitting around Fred and Jocelyn's kitchen table, the group deputized Kendy to call Will's son and ask if he knew where Will was and how he was doing. Will's son's wife told Kendy that Will was in the hospital but that he was doing well and would be out in a few days' time.

About a week later, I called Will at the nursing home where he was convalescing. He'd been diagnosed with pneumonia but said he was on the mend. He told me, "Yesterday we had a sing-along, supposedly a treat. We sang 'How Much Is That Doggy in the Window?' Jesus Christ. Great material for a satirist here. Nursing homes." He said he was very touched that I called.

A few weeks later, I called him at home and asked if I could interview him again. He explained that he had both an occupational therapist and a regular therapist coming to visit him that day, so maybe another time would be better.

"Sounds like you're getting a lot of help," I said.

"It's like goddamned Grand Central in here. Every fifteen minutes there's someone knocking on the door asking me if I want their services, but the only one I could really use is that of a nineteen-year-old blonde."

"But, anyway . . ."

"But, anyway . . ."

I CALLED HIM BACK a few days later at the appointed time.

"I have a little trepidation about interviewing you again," I said, "given what happened last time."

"Trepid not."

I asked how he was doing vis-à-vis Mom, and he told me, "My life has been turned upside down. Thirty-six years together. She was my best friend. It's been a shocker. I'll love her till I die. I don't know what to do with myself. When I was divorced at thirty-eight, I had a lot that I could do. At seventy-eight, there're fewer possibilities."

I said I was sorry. He asked what I thought about the divorce, and I said what I'd said to Mom—that I hated to see them in pain and that a selfish part of me felt anxious and unmoored.

"Your mother's a very strong-willed woman," he said.

"She is. But she's like me in that we both put on a good face during crises, even though we're crumbling inside."

"Stiff upper lip."

"Yeah."

Will sighed and said, "I'll get through it somehow before I croak."

I asked about his health, and he called himself "frail but OK."

"But you're not feeling like you're at the end?" I asked.

"No, there's still a little more fuel in the tank."

He said he'd talked with both Kendy and JP and that he was particularly happy about talking with JP because she'd thanked him for teaching her boys to fly-fish.

"So you have a legacy," I said.

"Precisely."

He asked how Greg was, which I can't remember his ever doing before.

It felt good to talk with him, as if we were both siphoning off steam through a valve. I was reminded of the camaraderie of a conversation we'd had eight years ago. Will had been doing some consulting work that had necessitated a lot of travel, and the freelance writer in me had wondered how he was planning to charge his clients.

"Do you bill door to door?" I'd asked.

"Nooooo," he said, mock-gravely. "Pajama to pajama."

But inherent to the steam valve–like conversation we were having was my slight fear that we were dealing with topics that might, so to speak, burn us. Christmas was less than a week away, and I suspected that Will was probably going to spend it alone; I wasn't sure if I should ask about it.

When I finally did ask, my suspicion turned out to be wrong: "My son and his wife and my grandchild are coming for Christmas. They're gonna make a meal. I tried to tell them to stay home and have their own traditions. But they want to be with the old man."

———

WILL CALLED ME BACK the next day, saying he had a question about something I'd said.

"You mentioned something about your mother putting on a good face even when she's crumbling inside."

"Right," I said. "I just meant that she and I both do that when we're in crisis mode."

"Oh." Pause. "You didn't mean she's *still* crumbling inside?"

"No."

"OK."

"I think she's moved on."

"Right, right, that's what I thought you meant."

We shared an awkward pause. I didn't know what to do with it, other than to leave it.

"Lots of love to you, Will."

He breathed out a staccato blast of air, as if slightly impressed.

"I believe that," he said.

"You should."

{ 23. }

We try to stay afloat. We cling to the proverbial wreck-age. *Last Words: The Final Journals of William S. Burroughs* is a collection of diary entries that the *Naked Lunch* author and literary outlaw made from November 1996 to July 1997, just days before his death. Though these journals cover a lot of classic Burroughs concerns—morality, man's stupid-ity, U.S. drug policy, literature—the writer who emerges from these pages is ultimately a much more loving and optimistic one than we might expect. After all, Burroughs was a lifetime opiate addict who once sold heroin to support his habit; his books had been full of pederast fantasy and strangulation. He accidentally shot and killed his common-law wife during a drinking game in Mexico City, and he later specialized in a kind of painting in which he used a shotgun to propel paint onto canvases. In short, a man whose idea of fun did not incor-porate yarn or golfing.

The love and optimism in the late journals seems to be the end product of Burroughs's examination of his own mortality. Burroughs moved to Lawrence, Kansas, when he was sixty-seven and spent the last sixteen years of his life there. His health improved after a triple coronary bypass in 1991 although he was saddled with arthritis, a hiatal hernia, and the cataracts in both eyes that seemed only to heighten his pale, ghostlike appearance. He looked like the first scene of Hamlet.

Prior to moving to Kansas, he'd not been fond of cats—in fact, had even been cruel to them. But he was greeted in Kansas by several strays, and thus began an end-of-life infatuation. As James Grauerholz, Burroughs's manager and editor, explains in *Last Words*'s introduction, Burroughs "thought often [now] of the many people in his life who had died, and the cats seemed to represent them for him." In 1986, Burroughs published *The Cat Inside*, an appreciation in which he celebrates cats as "natural enemies of the State" and rails against dogs and their "vilest coprophagic perversions." He states in the book's introduction, "My relationship with cats has saved me from a deadly and pervasive ignorance." As his house started to emanate the fulsome aroma of cat excreta—at the height of his kitty stewardship in the mid-1990s, Burroughs was master to Ginger, Fletch, Calico, Mutie, Senshu, and Spooner—the methadone-taking junkie could be heard showering his little charges with verbal abuse: "Come here, you little whore, you little bitch!"

What's notable about these journals is how they foreshorten Burroughs's end-of-life movement from pitch-black to light gray. We get references to a codeine derivative called Eukodol, which Burroughs says "hits like a speedball, Kid." We get various examples of violence and veiled aggression. We get the information that Burroughs's life review has revealed to him many people whom he wished he'd put in their places. But gradually, as the end comes closer, Burroughs's worldview grows increasingly sunshiny, and in his last diary entry he tells us that the "only thing [that] can resolve conflict is love, like I felt for Fletch and Ruski, Spooner and Calico. Pure love."

The last eleven words of Burroughs's diary are:

Love? What is it?
Most natural painkiller that there is.
LOVE.

———

GRAHAM GREENE's last book was a diary of dreams he recorded over the last twenty-five years of his life, before dying at age eighty-six in 1991. As with Burroughs, the final work of this writer who was prone to pessimism, suicidal impulses, and dark-hued satire shows a surprisingly congenial world. The first dream that Greene writes about recounts a magical ride on a train filled with kind and jolly passengers ("I had never in my life felt such a sensation of happiness"), and the last dream sees Greene writing a poem in which he likens the imminence of his own death to the reassuring arrival of nursery tea.

Burroughs's and Greene's works suggest their authors' high lucidity at the time of writing. Other authors' late works have earned literature professor Barbara Herrnstein Smith's label "senile sublime." This term has been picked up by other theorists and authors, including Eve Kosofsky Sedgwick, who has written that it applies to "various more or less intelligible performances by old brilliant people, whether artists, scientists, or intellectuals, where the bare outlines of a creative idiom seem finally to emerge from what had been the obscuring puppy fat of personableness, timeliness, or sometimes even of coherent sense." In 2006, at the age of seventy-four, John Updike referenced both Smith and Sedgwick when he wrote, "Successful late works, shed of 'obscuring puppy fat,' tend to have a translucent thinness." In some instances, apparently, this thinness is literal: I think of the spindly, towering, and terrifying sculptures of spiders that the ninety-six-year-old sculptor Louise Bourgeois has been making for the past few decades. These freakishly attenuated creatures in bronze can be as tall as thirty feet, thus allowing their cowed beholders to scurry below them. The punchline is that Bourgeois has said that the sculptures are all about her mother.

Updike also pointed out that another aspect common to late works is the way they often deny death. Shakespeare's sonnets, published in 1609, seven years before the Bard's death at the age of fifty-two, play with this theme repeatedly:

> *Yet do thy worst, old Time: despite thy wrong,*
> *My love shall in my verse ever live young.*

In James Joyce's last novel, *Finnegans Wake*, published two years before its author's death in 1941, Finnegan awakes at his own wake.

What's going on here? Why the jettisoning of death honoring and puppy fat? Surely these two traits bespeak more than, in the case of the former, a last stab at immortality or, in the latter, an inability to flesh out ideas in full form. In "Art and Time," an essay in his 1971 book *Art and the Creative Unconscious,* psychologist Erich Neumann considers the late quartets of Beethoven, the late self-portraits of Rembrandt, the late plays of Shakespeare, and the late paintings of Titian; he says that they all exhibit a quality that he describes as "transcendent." He writes, "In these works of man a numinous world is manifested in which the polarity of outward and inward—nature and art—seems to be resolved . . . This art no longer relates either consciously or unconsciously to any historical time; the solitary monologue of these 'extreme' works is spoken, as it were, into the void . . . It is no longer oriented toward the world or man, the ego or the collective, security or insecurity; instead, the creative act which mysteriously creates form and life in nature as in the human psyche seems to have perceived itself and to shine forth with its own incandescence."

Kathleen Woodward—the University of Washington professor who declared a moratorium on wisdom some pages ago—has mined incandescence as well. In *At Last, the Real Distinguished Thing*, Woodward does a close reading of four late poems— T. S. Eliot's "Four Quartets," Ezra Pound's "Pisan Cantos," Wallace Stevens's "To an Old Philosopher in Rome" from *The Rock*, and book five of William Carlos Williams's "Paterson." Woodward looks at how, in confronting "the collapse of order" and seeking "to discover, or generate, a new ground of authority," each of these poets was able to bring a kind of closure to his life.

The four poems Woodward looks at are very different from one another, and not all four of her poets were old when they wrote them. Yes, Stevens and Williams were seventy-five when their last books appeared. But Pound—who'd spent six months in a prison camp in Pisa, Italy, during which time he translated Confucius and worked on "Pisan Cantos" and spent three weeks in a reinforced steel cage—was only sixty-three. Eliot was only in his mid fifties, but his "voice and theme," Woodward writes, "are definitely that of an older man." (Eliot, it should be pointed out, was so somber as a young man that he sometimes put powder on his face to make himself look even grayer than he was.) Nevertheless, the four poems share similar qualities: an affirmative vision; a more pronounced lyric quality than in most of the poets' other work; personalism; a meditative mode; and a striving for "transcendence of historical time, seeing history, as Eliot does in 'Little Gidding' as 'a pattern / Of timeless moments.'"

Though each of the four poets asserted his own definition for the term, they all pay homage in these late poems to the concept of the "still point." Eliot addresses it the most directly of the four, writing, "Except for the point, the still point / There would be no dance, and there is only the dance"—and this is in a poem that famously tells us that, at the end of our exploring, we will arrive back at our starting point and "know the place for the first time."

Over the years, the idea of the still point has been used to describe the reconciliation of opposites or a desire for wholeness; the term has popped up in the fields of Zen, Surrealism, poetry, and tai chi. Poet Octavio Paz thought it was the center of poetry: "The opposites do not disappear, but are fused for an instant. It is a little like suspended animation: time has no importance." André Breton wrote, in the *Second Manifesto of Surrealism*, "Everything tends to make us believe that there exists a certain point of the mind at which life and death, the real and imagined, past and future, the communicable and the incommunicable, high and low cease to be perceived as contradictions. Now, search as one may, one will never find any other motivating force in the activities of the Surrealists than the hopes of finding and fixing this point." And Herbert Blau contended, in an essay about tai chi: "All is still at the still point of the turning wheel. The circular movement activates all the dark and light forces of human nature. Mutability and mortality."

In the place where opposites collide and we literally lose all sense of time, we find unity and a kind of communion. Woodward writes, "We no longer encounter the careful impersonality of the poet that was the hallmark of much early American Modernism. Nor do we find the irony that imposes distance. Instead, there is a new closeness, a more open dialogue between the poet and himself and between the poet and the reader."

Hits like a speedball, Kid.

AND WHAT OF our more mundane moods and needs at the end of life? We don't all, like poets and great artists, traffic in the sublime. Though it can be difficult to generalize about how we all face our last days on earth, anecdotal evidence suggests that,

→ in the clinches, many of us become more like ourselves than ever. "There are surprises," psychologist and author Mary Pipher writes, "but generally people take all their strengths, skills, attitudes, into the country of old-old age."

The imminence of death and the net result of life review can yield a small flurry of activity—regrets may be expressed, requests made, wills redrawn, memories rekindled. But in general, it's interesting to see how people, when preparing to leave this earth, act quintessentially. I once saw a documentary about the last-meal requests made by prisoners on death row, and laughed out loud when I learned of one request for low-fat salad dressing.

Look at how some seniors talk about their own funerals. Ninety-five-year-old rabble-rouser Studs Terkel told a *Chicago Tribune* reporter that he wants his ashes mixed with his wife's and then scattered in Chicago's Bughouse Square, "the patch of park across from the Newberry Library, where he spent many of his formative years, wide-eyed at the words pouring from the assortment of lunatics, philosophers, intellectuals, and radicals who got up on soapboxes to speak." Breaking out into a gleeful grin, Terkel told his interviewer, "Scatter us there. It's against the law. Let 'em sue us."

Or consider Mathilda Jones, a feisty ninety-eight-year-old maiden who told the *Houston Chronicle* in 1987 that she wanted no male pallbearers at her funeral: "If men could not invite me out when I was alive, they're not going to carry me out when I'm dead."

People's last words, too, often bespeak a crystallization of self. Though a surprisingly large percentage of last words, according to Mary Pipher, are "I love you" or "thank you," some folks individuate themselves. The iconoclasm of playwright Henrik Ibsen, who spent most of his career scandalizing Victorian morality with his plays such as *Hedda Gabler* and *A Doll's*

House, extended even to his 1906 deathbed. When Ibsen's nurse remarked that Ibsen was looking better, Ibsen commented, "On the contrary," and promptly died.

Or take Socrates. He's imprisoned and about to drink the hemlock that will kill him—it's a moment wherein one might be tempted to cling to the immortality of the soul or to comfort oneself or one's loved ones. But Socrates—who, you'll remember, was the first person to systematically inquire into the nature of wisdom and who, in testing the oracle's pronouncement, had determined that he, Socrates, was paradoxically wise because he knew he was not—took the high ground even in his dying words: "Remember, in this argument, I am only seeking to convince myself. Do but see how much I have to gain if the immortality of the soul is proved. If it is true, then I do well to believe it. And if there is nothing after death, my ignorance will do me no harm. This is the state of mind in which I approach our argument. I would ask you to be thinking of the truth, and not of Socrates."

Others' last words follow suit:

William H. Vanderbilt, president of the New York Central Railroad, who died in 1885, said, "I have no real gratification or enjoyment of any sort more than my neighbor down the block who is worth only a half million."

Benito Mussolini told his executioners, "Shoot me in the chest!"

John Barrymore said, "Die? I should say not, dear fellow. No Barrymore would allow such a conventional thing to happen to him."

Henry James said, "So here it is at last, the distinguished thing."

James Thurber said, "God bless. God damn."

Gertrude Stein asked Alice B. Toklas, "What is the answer?" and then, when Toklas didn't respond, laughed and said, "In that case, what is the question?"

Flo Ziegfeld said, "Curtain! Fast music! Lights! Ready for the finale! Great! The show looks good! The show looks good!"

Timothy Leary said, "Why not? Yeah."

Gary Gilmore told a firing squad, "Let's do it!"

Anna Pavlova said, "Get my swan costume ready."

Saddam Hussein said, "There is no God but Allah, and Muhammad is God's messenger."

P.T. Barnum said, "How were the receipts today at Madison Square Garden?"

The Indian chief Crowfoot said, "A little while and I will be gone from you. From whither I cannot tell. From nowhere we come, into nowhere we go. What is life? It is the flash of a firefly in the night. It is the breath of a buffalo in the wintertime. It is the little shadow which runs across the grass and loses itself in the sunset."

Buddha said, "Decay is inherent in all things."

Joan Crawford, seeing her housekeeper praying, said, "Damn it . . . Don't you dare ask God to help me."

What comes through when you read a lot of people's dying words is the inimitableness of so many of these last gasps; you could remove the names from some of these quotes and we'd still know who said them. The image of Oscar Wilde languishing in a cheap hotel and uttering "Either the wallpaper goes or I do" is so on the nose as to be almost self-parodic. It is, you'll forgive me, dead-on.

––––––

WHAT PROMPTS THESE STATEMENTS, be they of the common "I love you" stripe or of the more exotic "Here is an enigmatic koan that throws my lifetime's accumulation of triumphs and disasters into dramatic high relief" stripe? Is it possible to generalize?

Eager to find out, I called *How We Die* author Sherwin Nuland at Yale and I asked, "Is it possible to generalize about what people in critical care or on their deathbeds are thinking about?"

"That's a very, very difficult question. It's never been addressed in any systematic way," he told me. "But I think we should not under any circumstances underestimate the role of fear. Fear which we never much talk about. That's one of the motivating factors."

"Fear of death?"

"Fear of death. Fear of nonexistence. This concept of nonexistence: 'The world will go on, and I will not be there' is a terrifying phenomenon to face. This is one of the reasons why I think it's so important to reassure people that although the world will physically go on without them, that they have left a heritage or legacy. They've left something of value, and that part of that is love."

"Is this what you meant in *How We Die* when you wrote that 'in the care of advanced disease, hope should be redefined'?"

"Yes. When I was in medical school, I was taught that one should never let a patient lose hope. But how do you define hope when in the usual sense there is no hope for survival? I always like Václav Havel's definition of hope, which is not that something will come out well but that something will make sense. And what makes sense for a person who is close to death? Or who has to face the inevitability of death? One of the things is a kind of promise. A promise that we'll never leave him, the promise that we'll accompany him through whatever he must go through, right to the very end. Another is to convey to people who are close to us how much their lives have meant to us. We also have to somehow reassure people that we will not worsen their suffering by ill-advised attempts to try some new technology or make some new diagnostic maneuver. But most importantly, the hope for what we might term immortality—how they have changed our lives. How we have achieved certain wisdom because of our relationship with them."

AND SO WE SEE how the emotional and psychic stakes of the deathbed can grow sky-high. The dying—their medical condition aside—may be in the throes of fear, and their loved ones may be laboring to offer reassurance and meaningful acknowledgment of the dying person's existence. Against this backdrop of swirling psychosocial foment can sometimes emerge that most dramatic of occurrences, the deathbed confession.

At the moment, the phrase "deathbed confession" bespeaks the hackneyed, made-for-televison drama desperate for third-act payoff—a grizzled octogenarian character actor reveals the true paternity of our heroine, emitting Emmy-caliber warmth and resignation.

Indeed, many of the deathbed confessions one hears about are or have been dismissed as lore. For instance, some think that Darwin renounced his theory of evolution on his deathbed, but it's far more likely that he merely expressed concern over some of his youthful speculations. The chaplain of Saint Francis Hospital in Hartford claimed that he brought the poet Wallace Stevens into the Catholic fold on his deathbed in 1955; but Wallace had long argued that God should be spelled with a lowercase "g" and did not have a church funeral. More recently, Bob Woodward claimed in his book *Veil* to have visited the sedated former CIA director William Casey on his deathbed in 1987 and asked if Casey had known about the diversion of Iran arms-sale proceeds to the Nicaraguan Contras; Casey supposedly nodded his head in confirmation. Robert Kaiser, the *Washington Post*'s assistant managing editor for national affairs, said of this, "It's a profoundly ambiguous scene. Here's a guy who had a brain tumor, and it's the only question Woodward gets to ask him, and his answer is a nod. It isn't what a newspaper editor would regard as confirmation of an extremely sensitive news story."

But there have been, of course, any number of legitimate and fully authenticated confessions. Professional model maker Christian Spurling, age ninety and near death, confessed that he had built the model—from plastic wood and a submarine bought at a Woolworth's outside London—of the Loch Ness monster that we see in the famous, blurry photograph. On his deathbed in 2000, British gangster Reggie Kray confessed to a previously unknown murder, though he failed to fully apologize for his violent career, saying only, "But I suppose if I've been a bit too violent over the years I make some apologies about it, but there's little I can do about it now, so again, it's no good reflecting. It's pointless, negative."

What prompts these revelations—or, for that matter, the confession of Günter Grass, at age seventy-nine in 2006, that he was a formerly a member of the SS, or Mark Felt's confession to *Vanity Fair*, in 2005 at age ninety-one, that he was Deep Throat? Grass, when asked why he had confessed after hiding his ties to the SS from everyone except his wife, told one German newspaper, "It weighed on me. My silence during all these years is one reason that led me to write this book. It had to come out." And, according to the *Vanity Fair* article, Felt's family persuaded him to fess up so that they could parlay the resultant book and media deals into money for the education of Felt's grandchildren. Additionally, the family didn't want Felt to pass on only to have Bob Woodward reveal his identity and then bask in the glory.

But in most cases of sudden late-in-life revelation, it would be presumptuous to try to articulate the motivating factors—outside, of course, those pressures exerted by the Catholic Church. The *Catholic Encyclopedia* tells us, "So far as priestly assistance goes the first step in the process of preparation for death is receiving of the patient's confession and the conferring of sacramental absolution. Indeed, inasmuch as it offers the ordinary means of reconciliation with God, it is the most indispensable factor in helping the soul to qualify for its departure from the body."

It's probably safe to say that the trait that Nuland told me that we bring to our final moments—fear—mixes with a lot of other traits, among them guilt, shame, anger, pride, a sense of justice or reckoning, and perhaps even egotism or a desire to make one last stab at immortality. This last motive gains credence from the fact that some confessions—like Grass's or Woodward's Casey one—are tied to the publications of books.

There are three deathbed confessions, though, wherein we have enough information that we can speak with more certainty than usual about motivation or cause. I preface the first by stating that it is unclear whether it even is a deathbed confession or merely a deathbed statement. I refer to the dying words of gangster Dutch Schultz in 1935, which is the deathbed confession that has been the object of the most interest and speculation because it is thought to contain clues to the whereabouts of a steel box containing bonds, diamonds, and cash worth about fifty million dollars. The box is thought to be buried on the banks of the Esopus Creek in the small Catskills town of Phoenicia. Though there's a lot of murkiness surrounding the treasure and its location, it's nevertheless fairly clear that Schultz's famously incoherent ramblings were the queer offspring of his 106-degree fever and a lot of morphine. Shot in the stomach by two Murder, Inc., hitmen while urinating in a men's room at the Palace Chophouse in Newark, New Jersey, Schultz was rushed off to the hospital one October night. Schultz's statement, taken down by a Newark police stenographer, sounds almost like Samuel Beckett. I condense:

> Please make it quick, fast and furious . . . I don't want harmony. I want harmony. Oh, mamma, mamma! Who give it to him? Who give it to him? Let me in

the district-fire-factory that he was nowhere near. It smoldered. No, no. There are only ten of us and there are ten million fighting somewhere of you, so get your onions up and we will throw up the truce flag . . . The sidewalk was in trouble and the bears were in trouble and I broke it up. Please put me in that room. Please keep him in control. My gilt edged stuff and those dirty rats have tuned in . . . Oh, sir, get the doll a roofing. You can play jacks and girls do that with a soft ball and do tricks with it. I take all events into consideration . . . I am half crazy. They won't let me get up. They dyed my shoes. Open those shoes. Give me something. I am so sick . . . Police, mamma, Helen, mother, please take me out. I will settle the indictment. Come on, open the soap duckets. The chimney sweeps. Talk to the sword. Shut up, you got a big mouth! Please help me up, Henry. Max, come over here. French-Canadian bean soup. I want to pay. Let them leave me alone.

The motivating force behind the second confession—that of Anatole Broyard, who was the daily book critic for *The New York Times* in the 1970s and 1980s—was discrimination. The son of light-skinned New Orleans Creoles, Broyard passed himself off as white—this practice is referred to as *passablanc*—all his adult life. He had black hair, olive skin, and Gallic features. Although he worked in a field that presumably wouldn't have discriminated against him—and indeed, might even have promoted him on the basis of his minority status—Broyard didn't want to be labeled a "Negro" writer and, at some level, realized that it's easier to be white than black in America. But, just before his death from cancer in 1990, Broyard labored to tell his two children his secret. (His wife had to be the one to say, "Your father is part black," when her husband was unable to deliver the goods.)

His story was later recounted in nonfiction books by his daughter, Bliss, and historian Henry Louis Gates, as well as being the basis for the Philip Roth novel *The Human Stain*.

The third example, like that of Dutch Schultz, also takes a liberal interpretation of the term "deathbed confession." One day in 1974, Tom DeFrank, a reporter at *Newsweek* who was covering Gerald Ford, found himself alone with the vice president. (Ford's press secretary had fallen asleep next door.) Grousing about Nixon loyalists who thought Ford wasn't being supportive enough of his boss, Ford told DeFrank, "Dick Nixon knows I've been loyal. Why do they do this?" DeFrank responded that Nixon supporters were angry because Nixon was finished and Ford would be his successor. Probably inspired by DeFrank's candor, Ford blurted out, "You're right. But when the pages of history are written, nobody can say I contributed to it." Suddenly realizing that such a statement, were it published, might start off a firestorm, Ford said, "You didn't hear that," walked around his desk to DeFrank, grabbed his necktie, and said he couldn't leave until they reached an understanding. A tense silence ensued, broken by Ford, who said, "Write it when I'm dead." DeFrank went on to cover Ford's brief presidency and his unsuccessful 1976 bid to retain the job; in 1991, he began conducting interviews with Ford, to be published only after Ford's death.

Published in October 2007, the interviews proved to be full of juicy and slightly bilious nuggets. For instance, when the former president had been asked in public about Bill Clinton, Ford simply said that he had voted for Senator Robert Dole for president in 1996; but he told DeFrank, "He's sick—he's got an addiction. He needs treatment . . . A lot of men have gone through treatment with a lot of success. But he won't do it because he's in denial." Ford said that Clinton and his allies asked him to help head off impeachment charges in 1998, but that Ford said he would not unless Clinton admitted he had lied to a grand jury about the Monica Lewinsky affair. Ford also used the protection of posthumous publishing to say that Ronald Reagan "had a helluva flair" but was "not up to the standards of either Democrat or Republican presidents." He doubted whether Dick Cheney was an asset to President Bush. As for Jimmy Carter, the man who quashed his presidential bid, "I think he's the weakest president I've ever seen in my lifetime."

While the motivating causes of Schultz's, Broyard's, and Ford's confessions—morphine and high fever, discrimination, and a backroom deal—are disparate, it's not a stretch, I think, to say that fear is lurking at the heart of all three of them. More specifically, the fear of being discovered or caught out.

AND WHAT CAN WE LEARN about the end of life from people who've had the ultimate end-of-life-experience—i.e., people who've died and come back? As with dreams, not everyone remembers their near-death experiences, but it's thought that about 25 to 30 percent do. Kenneth Ring, a professor of psychology at the University of Connecticut at Storrs who has studied near-death experiences (NDEs) since 1976, says that one out of three people who come close to death will have transcendental experiences. This experience will involve "a pattern of feeling and images and sensations which include a sense of the most profound peace and well-being that it is possible to imagine," Ring told *The New York Times* in 1988. "It's a sense of being separate from the physical body and sometimes being able to see it as though a spectator off to one side or from up above."

These feelings—probably prompted by a surge of endorphins, the hormones that act on the central nervous system to reduce pain, as evidenced in a "runner's high," and that may cause hallucinations—sound intense. Kevin Nelson, a University of

Kentucky neurophysiologist, told *AARP* magazine in 2007, "It's very likely that REM sleep and the arousal system of the brain are contributing to NDEs." He said that people with NDEs have "a different brain switch," which blends sleep with wakefulness and reduces the trauma of dying to a dreamlike state. People who have NDEs report a sensation of being bathed in golden light; traveling disembodied through a dark tunnel; coming in contact with an energy source that strikes them as divine; floating over a field of yellow flowers; joyful "reunions" with deceased loved ones with whom they communicate telepathically; and sorrow about having to return to the real world. Stranger yet are the changes that occur when these folks come back to earth. "People become life appreciators," Ring has said. "They don't care about success, fame, or fortune." Indeed, there are documented cases of people who, after their NDEs, adopt less materialistic lives, changing careers and becoming nurses, social workers, and volunteers. Many are said to have lost their fear of death.

A certain amount of the NDE research strikes me as bullcrap; I for one am hard-pressed to believe that eight million Americans have had NDEs, given that I've never crossed paths with a single one of these folks. But even if some of these findings are exaggeration—when, by contrast, English philosopher Sir Alfred J. Ayer, a noted atheist, had a NDE in 1988, he went only so far as to say that it "slightly weakened my conviction that my genuine death, which is due fairly soon, will be the end of me, though I continue to hope that it will be"—it's interesting to note their tenor and the movement they describe away from egoism. It's a movement we see repeated over and over, even in those instances that have a darker cast to them than those involving bright lights and fields of yellow flowers. May Sarton, the poet and lesbian whose journals are a staple of books about elders, wrote in her sixties, "The joys of my life have nothing to do with age. They do not change. Flowers, the morning light, music, poetry, silence, the goldfinches darting about." But in her seventies, after she'd had a stroke and had aged significantly, Sarton wrote, "I am learning that any true cry from the heart of an old person creates too much havoc in the listener and is too disturbing, because nothing can be done to help the person on the downward path."

Author and critic Susan Sontag, whose polemics and brazen intellectualism were the product of a mountainous self-confidence and an utter absence of self-irony, told her son throughout her battle with the myelodysplastic syndrome that killed her at age seventy-one in 2004, "This time, for the first time in my life, I don't feel special."

Or, as Eliot wrote in "Four Quartets," "The only wisdom we can hope to acquire / Is the wisdom of humility: humility is endless."

24

As it turns out, there's a book that changed the way I think about death, but it's not by T. S. Eliot, and it's not by Elisabeth Kübler-Ross or William Burroughs nor any poet or writer. It's a book of postmortem photography called *Sleeping Beauty.* These are black-and-white photographs of dead Americans, taken between 1843 and 1925.

The ghostly pale subjects of this book, not a few of whom are children, are dressed up in their Sunday best. Most of the subjects' eyes are closed, but occasionally you'll get an opened eye; these opened eyes brim over with exhaustion, bewilderment, or stunned awe.

The photographing of corpses was a common practice in nineteenth- and early-twentieth-century America. Much effort and pride went into these photographs, which were hung in homes and sent to relatives or sometimes fitted into lockets or pocket mirrors. Often, the photographs were the only ones ever taken of their subjects.

The first time I found this book on Greg's bookshelf, I stared at it with the benumbed fascination of a tourist. About half the subjects are shown in their coffins, and so my first pass through the book involved a lot of coffin cross-referencing—some of the caskets looked simple and cozy, while others looked slightly grandiose and daunting. I remember looking at plate 28, "Man Sitting in a Chair with a Book"—like all the pictures, it's grainy and black-and-white, but it differs from most of the others in that the man is fully dressed and, as the title indicates, seated, not recumbent. The model is also arresting because he has a strange overbite that is more than a little vampiric; I gazed at him and thought, Maybe he bit himself to death. In retrospect, this reaction of mine seems fairly patent—the only way for me to look at these pictures was to try to leaven the experience.

When I looked at the book again a short while later, I thought, Coooool, how creepy. I was interested this time in how some of the adult corpses looked like babies. I was also drawn to the graphic horror of plate 66, "The Murdered Parsons Family"— Mom, Dad, and three little children, all having sustained some head wounds, now stretched out on a big bed—and to the strange juxtapositions in plate 38, "Charlie—A Boy and His Toys," and plate 55, "Child and His Rocking Horse." Something about the implied movement and joy of playthings, when placed directly next to a dead body, caught me short.

The next time I thought to look at the book, I started to pull it off the shelf and then immediately put it back. I thought, No, this is creepy. Either the images themselves were creepy or my wanting to look at the images was creepy. I wasn't sure which.

Then I started telling my friends about the book and showing it to them. Their reactions—"Oh, that *is* creepy"—struck me as knee-jerk. They were reacting as if the pictures were some sort of macabre science project. No, no, I was tempted to say, you don't understand, these pictures are . . .

Are what? I didn't have a word. Not "historical," exactly, as that implied a detachment on the viewer's part that seemed a little antithetical to the images' visceral punch. And not "interesting" or "unusual," though they certainly were.

Over the months, not being able to put my finger on the right word kept pulling me back to the pictures. More specifically, I couldn't stop looking at the three pictures of plate 47, "Baby Dead from Dehydration, Three Poses." These show an emaciated infant holding a sprig of evergreen; were it not for the tininess of its body, this skeletal creature could just as easily be a hundred years old as one year old. The baby's eyes are open; glazed, these marble-like orbs stare off into the middle distance. They project an air of humble submission that is devastating. I twice found myself staring at these pictures and experiencing a slight numbness or buzz. I didn't understand this reaction until I realized that to look at these pictures is to be taken outside of time. It's not 1885 when I look at them, nor is it 2008.

If it is the covert mission of great works of art to take their viewers out of the here and now and deliver them to the gates of the eternal, then these photographs can be categorized as great works of art. They get at something larger than man or words could ever conjure. They show that, in death, the end has no end. The sculptor Jacques Lipchitz once said that "art is an action against death. It is a denial of death." And that is precisely what these pictures do. These deaths deny death. There is only one word for what these images are. They are beautiful.

25

D id I mention that I had been living all this time with a seventeen-year-old cat? (Please, reader, keep reading.) He and Greg had moved into my apartment a year before my wisdom research got rolling. This ungainly, low-to-the-ground Siamese fellow had been a groomer of human heads—he liked to reach for your head with his right paw and then, once he had you bent over in his clutches, lavish the crown of your head with his tongue for a period lasting between one and twelve minutes. His tiny, sandpapery ministrations fell somewhere between a kiss and a buffing; imagine having a very gentle manicure performed just inches from your face. If you tried to wiggle away, Hot Rod sank his claws more firmly into your scalp, even to the point of drawing blood.

Unlike the grooming sessions of other cats, whose affections are timed, however slyly or manipulatively, to feedings, Hot Rod's happened on their own schedule. And he lavished our heads with such rhapsodic intensity that you could hear it from other parts of the apartment; the snorfling, pig-drunk intake of his breath sounded like a very old or possibly homemade vacuum cleaner.

I asked Greg to write down some of his thoughts, and he offered,

> Hot Rod avoided the cat clichés: wary defensiveness, hyperalertness to threat. He had no defenses, never anticipated trouble. At times I would stagger into the house bearing a box of books or thirty pounds of laundry; any other cat would have fled, but Hot Rod would wander into my path and look up with mild curiosity, heedless of imminent trampling. He expected life to caress him, and it did. (That is, I did, all the time.) On many occasions he fell asleep while resting his head in the palm of my hand.

This cat was not always thus. Formerly rambunctious and roguish, he'd had his love button pushed halfway through his life, after the death of his colleague, Ed. Hot Rod had always been the assistant cat until, with the demise of the more assertive Ed, he assumed the corner office. Greg wrote,

> Hot Rod was the runt of his litter, and at the beginning of his life stupidity vied with cuteness as his primary characteristic. In his wild youth, he attacked bare feet and chased shoelaces and Super Balls. As he settled into maturity, with its attendant corpulence, he discovered the superior satisfactions of inertia. If a pigeon had perched on his head, he might have waited patiently for it to fly away. The intent urgency with which other cats track the movement of birds, squirrels, insects, and unfamiliar humans translated in Hot Rod to an urgent need both to provide and to receive affection. He never looked more distraught than when he wanted to plant himself next to me on a sofa that was too scattered with papers and books for him to mount. Some animal behaviorists might say that he

attached himself to me only because I fed him, but
that wouldn't account for his constant goal, regardless
of whether a meal was in the offing, to plop his large,
soft body against mine, preferably wrapping himself
around my head.

Yes, Hot Rod's impulses as a service provider were at odds
with the increasing bulbousness and ungovernment of his sil-
houette as he aged; over the years, this guy—who weighed in at
twenty-one pounds at his largest—was likened to, variously, an
eggplant, a burlap bag, a hedgehog, a haggis, Jabba the Hut, *Lord
of the Rings*'s Treebeard, Buddha, Leontyne Price, a Pakistani
deliveryman, a Rorschach blotch, an occluded weather front,
Shelley Winters, the outdoors, and a tuna.

The wisdom here lay in Hot Rod's innate sense of reciprocity: in being our apartment's prime purveyor of Love Without
Borders, he also unwittingly became the chief recipient of same.
I'm a wintry WASP, but in the thrall of Hot Rod's affection, I
became pure goo. I have made protestations of love to this little
homunculus that I would blush to recount; I have lain in beds
in hotel rooms in other countries, folded a spare pillow till it assumes a Hot Rod–esque shape, and then clutched it till daybreak.
What fuels my ardor is the fact that I have literally never met another creature who expresses pleasure as fully as he did. When
you petted his cheeks, his eyes became unfocused and dazed, as
if he had just downed a fifth of Night Train. The pulsing and
clutching of claws that's common to cats was briefly suspended.
The rightmost of the four pads of his back right foot drifted a
quarter of an inch away from the other pads in the manner of a
hitchhiker or mitten. His head slowly canted first to one side,
then the other, in bobbleheaded slow motion. You could almost
see a blurred circle of animated-cartoon cuckoo birds orbiting
his head.

There were variations of intensity here, too—one time, when he was standing on his two front paws, and looked particularly sozzled from my having rubbed his cheeks, he released, or had released, the weight from his legs and collapsed with a soft thud on the bed. On finding himself seated, he blinked and tried to look as if nothing had happened.

———

GREG: "Can there be wisdom in the absence of intellect? No one would claim that Hot Rod was a thinker; he didn't possess that other generic attribute of cats, craftiness. It's probably debatable whether any cat could be said to be really self-aware. But surely the absence of fear and the unfailing ability to find joy in the present moment are two attributes of an enlightened soul. He was a spiritual teacher whether he knew it or not."

One oft-quoted saying from a Zen Buddhist master runs, "When I eat, I eat; when I walk, I walk; when I sleep, I sleep." During a retreat open to the public at the Zen Mountain Monastery in Mount Tremper, New York, a few years ago, one visitor, tired of the theoretical discussion, asked somewhat sarcastically, "So tell me, is there a Zen attitude toward fucking?" Without missing a beat, the monastery's abbot responded, "When fucking, just fuck." For Hot Rod, it was always one thing at a time. This singleness of purpose is, of course, common to most animals and can be said to be one of animals' chief traits. But some animals take their commonality more seriously than others. Don't try to stop their head-licking, or it will end in bloodshed.

———

HOT ROD stopped eating on a Wednesday. Over a period of two months, he'd been throwing up once every couple of days. Fluid oozed from his left eye now, describing a stream of mucusy gunk down the side of his snout like a slow-motion teardrop.

He wheezed and tottered on his weak legs. He was a snuffly dinosaur.

Greg took him to the vet and returned with lots of syringes and saline solution. We were meant to give Hot Rod shots twice a day.

As Hot Rod's condition worsened, the apartment felt increasingly becalmed. It was eerily quiet, too—the groomer of human heads had taken down his shingle.

By Saturday, Hot Rod was so weak that he was stumbling. At one point he got his legs stuck in the crevasse between two of the pillows of the couch, and Greg had to airlift him to the floor. There, Hot Rod puddled as if boneless.

Greg said, "I'm tempted to skip the shots and just let him go in peace."

"It might be time."

Greg made an appointment at the vet's for 2:00 p.m. We had a long-standing dinner date at my friend Rory's house that night. Because Greg and I had been in such a funereal state for four days now—Greg's eyes had sprung a leak this Saturday morning, and if the stereo in the living room wasn't wafting out Barber's "Adagio for Strings," it is in my memory—it occurred to me that a little blast of social interaction might not be a bad thing to lift the gloom. For me, at least. I realized Greg probably wouldn't want to go, though, so I told him that I was going to call Rory, tell her about Hot Rod's situation, and say that I, but probably not Greg, would still like to come over, if only for a little while. Greg approved the plan. I wondered if I was being selfish here. I'd just talked to Mom and Kendy on the phone the night before, and I was thinking about how each of them would handle this situation. Mom would definitely go to the dinner party, I decided, but Kendy would probably not.

I went out and bought lilies and two cans of split-pea soup.

We put the lilies in a vase. We ate the soup in silence.

"I just thought of that old George Carlin line," Greg finally said, "that when you buy a dog, you're buying a tragedy."

We talked about how parents often give their kids pets to teach them about death, and I wondered if this isn't part of why adults have pets, too. Granted, the consolation and nonjudgmental love of pets is not to be beaten. But, to take the larger view, aged animals exist only in captivity, and thus man can be said to force both the inequities and the charms of aging on these adorable captives. Maybe at some subconscious level we have pets because, even as adults, we want to be reminded of the cyclical nature of life. Maybe to witness a loved one's passing—even if that loved one cannot speak and is so unevolved as to think that life's most profound aesthetic experience is eating kibble—is to allay our anxieties about our own deaths.

Or maybe we just really like the way our hair becomes matted as a result of copious licking.

———

THE VET was a thin, friendly woman in her early fifties, who wore sneakers.

She and Greg and I stood in the tiny operating room of her Greenwich Village office, the fluorescent light casting a slight blue sheen on the silvery-chocolate penumbral fur of the outstretched patient.

The vet gave Hot Rod a shot of Valium, waited five minutes, and then came back with a catheter.

"This is a barbiturate," she said. "It will anesthetize him and then deliver what is essentially an overdose."

Greg and I nodded our heads mutely. Overdose. Weird.

The vet started petting the patient and told us, "His breathing is really labored. I don't disagree with your decision."

I tried to parse the double negative but let it go.

She shaved a patch of one of Hot Rod's legs, then another, looking for a vein.

"You're a handsome boy," she cooed.

"He was a great cat," Greg said.

The vet nodded and said, "With a name like that, how could he not be?"

I stared at the patient and then at Greg and thought, These two have lived in nine different New York City apartments together.

Then my mind took a more selfish turn as I thought, During the time that I looked into the topic of old age, my mother's marriage exploded, my boyfriend's cat of seventeen years died, and I threw out my back. Can hip-joint replacement and Alzheimer's be far in the offing?

———

AFTERWARD, the vet said we could spend as much time as we wanted to with our guy. I asked if it was OK if I took a picture, and she said sure. I did and then gave Hot Rod a kiss good-bye.

I figured that Greg would want some time alone with the body, so I walked out into the lobby. The receptionist looked at me indulgently and meaningfully, as if to say, The loss of a pet is always really, really hard on the gays.

Greg and I walked home, Hot Rod's empty dark-green plastic carrying case swinging from Greg's arm like a meaningless purse.

———

SOMETIMES I WOULD REFER to Hot Rod as Le Tigre, and sometimes El Tiger, and once, in homage to the old *Saturday Night Live* sketch about the diner that serves only cheeseburgers, "*Tigre*burger, *Tigre*burger."

By meddling with the natural order of things, man has eliminated most of the predators and diseases that would otherwise have killed him. If it is not too presumptuous to ascribe motive to Mother Nature, we can say that she intended for us and our pets to die at much younger ages than we will—probably after we procreate. But we don't. We've achieved a degree of mastery over our circumstances. We have tamed the proverbial beast. And in so doing, we've granted ourselves the opportunity to age—to have achy bones and macular degeneration and mild nausea and body parts that seem to exist only in order to betray us.

Aging is an artifact of civilization. We've brought it upon ourselves. How will we shape its future? Will we nurture it and make it grow, as we've done with artifacts of civilization like architecture and poetry and medicine, or will we largely ignore it, as we've done with crime and alcoholism and illiteracy?

Whichever way we choose, there's a lot of sustenance and psychic fuel to be derived from a deeper appreciation of the phrase "cheat death." Because we're doing it every day.

{ 26. }

Adversity is wisdom's testing grounds. Just ask Althea Washington, a seventy-five-year-old retired schoolteacher who lost her husband and her house in Hurricane Katrina.

Althea and Bert had raised three kids in Pontchartrain Park, a quiet residential area in New Orleans' Upper Ninth Ward. Bert, a retired assistant principal, was an umpire and a referee for the sports teams at the high school where he worked; as Althea says, "That was his thing." And he loved it when the neighborhood kids came over to his and Althea's house to play on their swing set.

But in the beginning of 2005, Bert had a severe stroke, and Althea was forced to put him in a suburban nursing home about twenty minutes away from their house. At the onset of Hurricane Katrina, Althea got in touch with the nursing home, wondering if she should collect the oxygen-dependent Bert and move him to safer ground. But the nursing home encouraged Althea to join her younger son and his family who were evacuating New Orleans, so she did.

Once the storm had blown over and revealed its awful legacy—and once Althea could finally get a phone line through—she called the nursing home again. Bert had passed on. Althea was devastated.

Althea had heard that some Katrina victims were moving into Sun City, a senior apartment complex located on the edge of Houston in a small town called Jacinto City. With the financial assistance of FEMA, Althea settled in at Sun City. Shortly thereafter, she sent her son back to New Orleans to check on her house. His prognosis was grim. The nine-foot-high floodwaters had left the house a museum of mold. All Althea and Bert's possessions had been destroyed.

And then, as if life had not rained enough acrid misfortune down on this one woman, it delivered its final blow: Althea's insurance did not cover damage caused by "the peril of windstorm during a hurricane." There would be no money.

IN MY FIRST CONTACT with Althea, I explained my quest over the phone, telling her about some of the people I'd talked to. She said, "Mr. Alford, I'm just a quiet soul sitting here. I really don't have any wisdom for that caliber of reader you're talking about." I countered that I thought she was probably mistaken. We kept talking. She told me, "Our way of life is no more and never will be."

I asked about her apartment complex. Althea said Sun City was home to some 150 people, many of them Katrina and Rita evacuees. At this point, less than half of New Orleans' 85,000 elderly had returned to the city, according to the New Orleans Council on Aging. Althea's $650 monthly rent was heavily subsidized by FEMA, as long as she attended the group counseling sessions held on the premises. She said of the counseling, "It gives us a chance to vent. Some of us avoid it because we don't want to cry. I try not to cry. I just sort of soak it up." She elaborated, "I went to the store the other day and saw all these pretty suits, and I automatically thought, 'I don't need that, I've got a closet full of nice things.' And then I realized I don't even have a closet."

I sympathized. I allowed as how a cataclysm must be one of the greatest tests of one's faith.

"God calls all of us," the lifelong Methodist congregant told me. "There is a season to burn and a season to die. We accept that as faith. But there's an inner something in me that says, 'You're gonna be all right.' You surround yourself with people who also have faith."

She told me that her husband was buried about twenty-five minutes away from Sun City.

"I had to lay my husband in a foreign land. I couldn't do it in New Orleans because of the flooding. That put us in a bind. It took a while to find his body. Then it took about a month to get him here. It was a long process. It took something out of me. But what I tell myself is, At least Bert was not in the water. At least he did not pop up as an unknown. And when he saw me last, he knew I cared. That keeps me going."

I tried to formulate a response but couldn't. Anything I might have said would have seemed trivial. I felt honored that she trusted me enough to tell me all this.

Althea broke the silence by sighing and saying, "But this single-bedroom apartment is quite comfortable. It's close to the train, but I don't mind that. Can you hear that train, Mr. Alford?"

I could hear the train.

"As long as it stays on its track," she said, "I'll stay on mine."

———

Sun City is a collection of very new-looking, pastel-covered buildings on the side of the highway. It's about a half mile from a Budweiser plant and fifteen minutes from downtown Houston. Hanging from an iron fence surrounding it was a banner advertising a "Grand Opening" long since expired; I looked for the nearby train tracks but didn't spot them.

I parked my car in front of a man-made pond and was surprised to see a woman whom I took to be Althea standing in front of a building. She was smiling and wearing an embroidered white cotton blouse.

"Mrs. Washington?" I asked.

"Please call me Althea," she said. "And let me hug you hello!"

A nimbus of soft, silvery white hair surrounds Althea's head like a crown; her blazing smile could light a small country. Heavyset, she moves her body through space with a confident grace.

As we walked to her apartment, she showed me the complex's large, characterless common rooms. They were filled with mostly black seniors huddled in groups and talking—imagine a dorm at Howard if no one had ever graduated.

Althea's apartment is cozy and dominated by her kitchen table and her TV; we sat at the former and immediately started yakking. I learned that she is the granddaughter of a Louisiana circuit preacher and the possessor of a wonderfully warm and crystalline singing voice.

I also learned that Althea had recently celebrated her seventy-fifth birthday.

"It was quiet," she said of this occasion, pouring us both a glass of water after I had declined both soda and a plate of chicken. "It was lovely. A little lonely. I could have gone to my daughter. But there comes a time in your life when you just want to be still, you just want to be reflective. I just want to sit in my chair and say, It's all right. It really is all right."

As we talked, Althea sang snatches of songs from time to time; indeed, after we'd spent about an hour together, I realized that she had already sung me four songs, mostly spirituals.

"You have a beautiful voice," I told her.

"As you can tell I have too much vibrato, and it trails off to nothing, which means I have a little breath problem."

Knowing that Althea had sung in the choir of her church in New Orleans, I asked if she did the same here, and she said no, but that she'd done it once since resettling. She told me, "I'd passed this church going to Wal-Mart and I thought, I'll go there. So I stopped by. I looked in the church and saw the backs of everybody's heads *and everybody was white!*"

I started laughing, and Althea (who is black) said, "My apologies." She continued, "I thought, What do I do now? Lordy, what a thing to do to put me out. I better run. But then I thought, I'll just sit in back, and when I hear the benediction, I'll hurry up and get out."

In the middle of the service, on hearing Althea's pipes, one of the women seated in the back—"The sweetest lady. That's a sweetheart," Althea said—took the new visitor by the arm and walked her up to the stage to join the choir.

I asked, "So you're not tempted to join them regularly?"

"No. I sing from the pews now. I don't want to admit to myself that there are things I can't go back to. Some of the members of my New Orleans choir have moved away, and some have passed on. We'll never be the same group again. I sing from the pews now."

————

I WONDERED, of course, whether Althea was planning to return to New Orleans. She said she was undecided. But then she added that one of her two sons had an accident when young and has been a ward of the state ever since. She said, "I'll tell you, dear, the only reason why I would want to go home is because of that young man. At some point he'll be sent to a group home, and after that he may come home. I don't want him to come home and find a strange man at the door."

She pointed out that she had established a good life for herself here in Jacinto City. She elaborated, "But unless God takes me quickly, I don't want to die here. Maybe I'm not supposed to know. We know of one instance in the building where a resident's door had to be knocked down. So when I get a funny feeling sometimes at night—that little drop in energy—I unlock my top lock."

I looked over at the lock and imagined Althea unfastening it.

I asked Althea what advice she would give people who find themselves in trying times. She said, "You have to give yourself the strength to just keep on. You may not call it God, but whatever you believe in, don't forsake it. What is it that makes you move in the direction that you move in, what is it that sustains you? Have you given it any serious thought? Is it the Bible? Is it your family? Is it your neighbor? If it is, when you go into your home and are alone, when it's just you, talking to you—some of us call it prayer, some of us call it meditation, some of us call it self-motivation. What do you call it? Whatever you call it, find it—that deep, deep strength that lifts you. And let it lift you. Because guess what? You can. You can. You can. Trust me. It'll happen."

Althea apologized for talking too much, but I told her not to stop.

She told me, "I've already prayed for you. I prayed that you will be satisfied because I'm not a famous person. I don't know anything. I can't do anything. I have not reached or achieved any great things. I don't have a classroom. I don't have an office. I don't have a doctorate, or a master's degree. I just have a few hours above a bachelor's degree. It's with this inadequacy that I let you into my life. Unknown name, unknown number. But I welcome you as a caring gentleman. I listened to your voice when you called, and I thought, I don't hear control, I hear request. I said, Well, Lord, if it can help somebody, sure."

Staring down at the floor because I didn't want her to see that she had moved me to tears, I thanked Althea for being so generous with her time. She said she didn't want to be "the man who sits by the side of the road" and then recited from memory

the poem "House by the Side of the Road," written by Samuel
Walter Foss in 1899:

Let me live in my house by the side of the road,
Where the race of men go by.
They are good, they are bad, they are weak, they are strong,
Wise, foolish—so am I.
Then why should I sit in the scorner's seat,
Or hurl the cynic's ban?
Let me live in my house by the side of the road
And be a friend to man.

Suddenly and unexpectedly put in mind of my conversation
with the senior citizen I'd talked to who'd had the least possible
in common with her—Yale professor Harold Bloom—I asked
Althea what she got out of all the poems and songs she knew by
heart. She said, "The spiritual 'Steal Away'? It keeps me out of
the psychiatrist's chair." Then she explained, "They pull you
out of whatever you're stuck in. They say, I'm not going to take
that pill. I'm not going to fill my head with all those pills. Now
if I get in a state where others are in control, then I have no
choice. But I don't think every time a person feels bad he needs
to take a pill. I think you need to release it in some manner.
All of us don't release our stress. But if I take a pill—when it
wears off, then what? Then what? The people in the drugstore
will have to fill another prescription. If they don't, they won't
get paid. And the people who made the pill—they need to get
paid, too."

The way to stay afloat, she said, is not to feel sorry for
yourself.

"Pity parties are free," she told me. "But they cost you
emotion."

EVEN THOUGH I'd originally suggested that we talk for an hour or two, we ended up talking for three and a half. At one point in the third hour—some time after the burst of the war song "Invictus" but before the smattering of "Steal Away"—Althea stood, walked toward the television, and picked up an eighteen-by-twelve-inch color photograph of her husband and brought it back to the kitchen table.

A sharp dresser, Bert is wearing a cap in the picture. His warmth seems to be kindled from pure fellow feeling.

"It's still a lonely route," she said. "I don't have anybody to hold my hand. How dare I even think that I should." Then, addressing the picture, she said, "Because I'm still grieving for you."

She smiled at him and brushed a piece of lint off the picture.

"Because the power was down, I couldn't get in touch," she told him. "We waited for you. I had to buy you clothes. We laid you out good."

———

THE NEXT DAY I drove six hours to New Orleans. I spent the night in the French Quarter, and then the next morning, using directions Althea had given me, I drove to Pontchartrain Park to see her house.

First settled in the 1950s, when it was still so rural that one early settler's father gave her a shotgun to help negotiate its potential terrors, Pontchartrain Park was celebrated by its founders in an ad that called it "one of the biggest, most luxurious Negro developments ever undertaken in the South." A product of segregationist thinking, Pontchartrain Park, with its golf course and huge park and leafy, suburban appeal can be viewed as both a step forward and a step backward.

Today the theme of reassembly permeated the expanse of modest homes; the neighborhood looked like a trade show for Tyvek wrap. Lots of homeowners were living in trailers parked on their lawns; the few who were visible outside their houses or trailers stared at me, making me feel like I'd been ejected from a spacecraft.

Althea's house has a brick façade and lots of pale-blue aluminum siding; all the doors and windows had been replaced with plywood. Part of the carport's roof sagged down to the ground, an elephant trunk in search of peanuts.

Getting out of my car, it suddenly occurred to me that my cellphone was in the car's glove compartment and that it would be interesting to talk to Althea while I walked around the house. So I called her.

"Hi, Althea. It's Henry."

"Where are you?"

"I'm standing in front of your house."

"Oh, my stars! Let me put my shoes on!"

I said sure and waited a few moments. And then a few more. And then a few more.

Oh, my God, it gradually dawned on me, *she thinks I'm in Houston.*

I hung up, waited a few minutes, and called her back.

When Althea picked up the phone, she was laughing. She said she'd run out into her parking lot and walked up to a white car like mine, thinking I was in it.

I apologized profusely.

"Oh, my stars!" she said. "I am embarrassed."

"No, *I'm* embarrassed! I'm so sorry."

Althea told me to forget it.

I added, "When you said, 'Let me put my shoes on,' I thought, That is *so eccentric*."

We laughed for about four minutes straight.

———

BACK IN HOUSTON the next morning, I called Althea to set up the lunch that we'd planned to have together on this, my last day in the area. But Althea sounded somewhat depressed and explained that she'd had an upsetting phone call from her daughter the evening before that would require her to work off some of her stress.

"I'll do my own little screaming," she said. "Can't turn on my TV loud enough."

I could tell that today was not a great day to meet. She corroborated this hunch—"I need to pull away sometimes. I don't make it to all my appointments. Sometimes I have to pull away and let people get upset with me. But I'm so happy to have had the opportunity to bend your ear a little. That's one of the blessings of making a new friend, and I think I have made one here."

NOW THAT I WASN'T MEETING ALTHEA, I had a few extra hours before going to the airport. I turned on the radio in my hotel room and packed my suitcase. I tried to do some writing. I read a magazine article. Then, idly looking for something to distract me, I found myself peering into the set of drawers directly under my room's telephone. Gideon's Bible. I hadn't looked at it since consulting it for my thumbnail history of wisdom a year or so earlier. Flipping to Ecclesiastes, I started reading. I quickly realized that I probably could not have chosen a more ironic section to read—Ecclesiastes is all about the futility of trying to grasp wisdom—"And I set my heart to know wisdom and to know madness and folly. I perceived that this also is grasping for the wind."

But as I read along, I saw echoes of many of the people I'd gotten to know in the preceding months.

I thought of Granny D: "Whatever your hand finds to do, do it with all your might, for there is no work or device or knowledge or wisdom in the grave where you are going."

I thought of Sylvia Miles: "So I perceived that nothing is better than that a man should rejoice in his own works, for that is his heritage. For who can bring him to see what will happen to him?"

I thought of Charlotte Prozan: "It is better to hear the rebuke of the wise than for a man to hear the song of fools."

I thought of Harold Bloom: "The excellence of knowledge is that wisdom gives life to those who have it."

I thought of Edward Albee: "Because for every matter there is a time and judgment, though the misery of man increases greatly."

I thought of Ram Dass: "A man's wisdom makes his face shine."

I thought of Althea Washington: "All things come alike to all: one event happens to the righteous and the wicked; to the good, the clean and unclean; to him who sacrifices and him who does not sacrifice."

Finding all these resonances was slightly eerie. I had a strange sensation that I was "meant" to be reading this particular book at this particular moment in my life. But Ecclesiastes' message is nothing if not ominous: although it maintains that looking for wisdom is part of a well-lived life, the search is futile because it's impossible to attach any meaning to wisdom. Also, everyone, wise and foolish alike, ultimately dies. All is vanity and grasping for the wind.

So, in the face of all this meaninglessness, what route does Ecclesiastes suggest we take? "Eat, drink, and be merry." Now, *that* I can do.

About a month later, I sent Althea a care package. She had twice mentioned in conversations that "cheese agrees with me," and so I sent her a four-cheese sampler from an online grocer.

When she called me to thank me, we talked for a while, and I was struck again by her quiet strength. Her situation remained the same: she wasn't sure if she would return to New Orleans. She still worried about her kids. She was still unlocking the top lock on her door.

But overall, her outlook was optimistic. She was doing what is probably the most challenging thing for any of us to do: living in good faith. Being in such close contact with other Katrina folk, some of whose situations were worse than her own, seemed to be giving her sustenance and context. Socrates once said, "If all misfortunes were laid in one common heap whence everyone must take an equal portion, most people would be contented to take their own and depart."

At one point during our conversation, I heard the train whistle blow in the background again. I knew more than ever that it would stay on its track.

I t occurred to me that there might be a more direct method to track down wisdom—a method that does not involve sitting in midtown restaurants or relying on the postal service to deliver unsuspected shipments of cheese.

I thought about the psychologist Gisela Labouvie-Vief. In experiments that she did in the 1970s, Labouvie-Vief demonstrated how seniors, when given problems to solve, sometimes discard hard-fact-based logic in favor of larger truths that they have arrived at through experience. In one experiment, older adults were told to arrange miniature houses on a simulated meadow, and then were asked if the arrangement of the houses would affect the amount of grass to be mown. Some of the test-takers did not supply the correct answer—that the configuration of the houses would not affect the square yardage of the lawn. However, they pointed out that if the houses were positioned close together, then the small, awkward patches of lawn would take more time to mow.

In another experiment, Labouvie-Vief had forty-five young men (average age 22.3 years) and forty-five older men (average age 74.2 years) listen to a fable, "The Wolf and the Crane," about a wolf who asks a crane to remove a bone lodged in the wolf's throat. The crane accomplishes the task and asks for a reward. The wolf tells him that the reward is to have survived putting his head down a wolf's throat. When the older men in Labouvie-Vief's experiment were asked to recall the story, their recollections were markedly different from the younger men's: they emphasized the story's larger, moral dimensions. One said, "The moral of the story as I understood it was that people should not seek a reward for their well doing, but be content with having done a good deed." When Labouvie-Vief and her colleagues switched the question to "recall as much as you can," the older men fared as well as the younger did in recounting factual details; but when they were given leeway, they'd emphasized the metaphorical. Labouvie-Vief wrote, "They insist on meaning. They are willing to sever form from context, to dissociate structure from function, to isolate thinking from its application."

This propensity for larger truths made me think of the work of David Greenberger. Greenberger had become an activities director at the Duplex Nursing Home in the suburbs of Boston in 1979. He started asking the forty-five residents of the all-male home questions about life and then published their answers in a photocopied newsletter called *The Duplex Planet;* he unearthed treasures like "If you are an old man and you go into a bar wearing pajamas, people will buy you drinks." Soon, hipsters like Jonathan Demme and Matt Groening and Michael Stipe were subscribing to Greenberger's zine. Greenberger went on to incorporate his charges' insights and witticisms into other media, including a documentary, a book, and lectures. I interviewed him in 1993, and he'd said of his subjects, "I'm trying to recast them as individuals."

Upon contemplating both the "Wolf and the Crane" findings and the pajamas-in-a-bar findings, I realized that aphorisms were the best vehicle for the kind of higher thinking that Labouvie-Vief and Greenberger had unearthed. After I'd written my thumbnail history of wisdom, my interest in these little nuggets of philosophy had continued to grow, leading me to a book called *The World in a Phrase: A Brief History of the Aphorism* by James Geary. Geary writes that "aphorisms must work quickly because they are meant for use in emergencies. We're most in need of aphorisms at times of distress or joy, ecstasy or anguish." In explaining why pithiness is next to godliness, Geary quotes from *The Cloud of Unknowing*, an anonymous fourteenth-century English monk's spiritual instruction manual:

> A man or a woman, suddenly frightened by fire, or death, or what you will, is suddenly in his extremity of spirit driven hastily and by necessity to cry or pray for help. And how does he do it? Not, surely, with a spate of words; not even in a single word of two syllables! Why? He thinks it wastes too much time to declare his urgent need and his agitation. So he bursts out in his terror with one little word, and that of a single syllable: "Fire!" it may be, or "Help!" Just as this little word stirs and pierces the ears of the hearers more quickly, so too does a little word of one syllable, when it is not merely spoken or thought, but expresses also the intention in the depth of our spirit.

Surely, I thought to myself as I was sitting at my desk one day, there are older folks out in the world who harbor some of this kind of information, be it of the pajama-wearing or the fire-cautioning stripe. Surely, the world is full of "elderisms."

Eager to find out, I wrote a two-hundred-word description of what I was looking for. I explained that I was in search of "short, philosophical, and possibly funny thoughts about life" from people seventy and older. I offered examples of two serious-minded sayings ("The best cure for sadness is to learn something" and "There is no later. Later is now") and two humorous ones ("A bag of assorted bagels with one garlic bagel in it is a bag of garlic bagels" and "We're all sisters under the mink").

I e-mailed the description to sixty-eight folks I'd been on the *Nation* cruise with, telling them to feel free to forward it; seven responses trickled in. Eighty-one-year-old Walt Ligon of Pentwater, Michigan, submitted, "Hope is stronger than experience," and Virginia Laddey, eighty-five, of Irvine, California, wrote, "Once again I was not consulted." A woman named Alix Dobkin wrote from Woodstock, New York, that her deceased father, Bill, had often opined, "People is animals, and them with feathers is boids," which I think we can all agree with. I was reminded of my research into the still point when John Glass of Los Angeles wrote, "There are many ways of moving forward but only one way of standing still."

Next, I started cold-calling senior centers and senior-friendly organizations across the country, hitting about sixty places in eleven states; I asked people to post my description on a Web site or a bulletin board. I also e-mailed the description to about twenty-five colleagues or friends. Over the course of two months, I received nineteen responses. A few of these came from people I knew or who were friends with someone I knew. My friend Jenny's mother's Italian teacher in Chicago, an ebullient woman named Tea Cetjin, told me, "Be careful of getting into the habit of anything." My ex's father, Jack Taylor of Monterey, California, wrote that his Appalachian mother used to say, "It'll all come out in the warsh" (apparently she also used to say, "It's darker than the inside of a black bull with his tail shut"—as Taylor explained, "Grandma was on the earthy side").

The larger share of the nineteen responses came from strangers, including three from sober-sounding men. John LaPlante, working for the Peace Corps in the Ukraine, opined, "To get a good look at yourself, take yourself far away." J. Adam Milgram of Sausalito wrote, "Our aging does not signal the end of our lives, but rather its fulfillment." Stan Kelly-Bootle of London quipped, "The Christian message is that good deeds are rewarded: you can't take it with you, but you can mail it ahead."

The person who sent in both "All martyrs are control freaks" and "All the wrong people have self-esteem" said s/he wished to remain anonymous. Judging by his/her submissions, I could only imagine that this person lives with a bipolar control freak who is by turns masochistic and vain. After printing out the e-mail, I scrawled on its margins, "Courtney Love's roommate?"

The most notable of these submissions, though, came from the Azusa Senior Center in California. I'd called the center's phone number, which I'd found on the Internet; activities director Heath Hamilton had picked up the phone. When I explained what I was looking for, Hamilton said, "I'll hand it off to our funny-sayings lady."

"You have a funny-sayings lady?" I asked, surprised.

"We do. She keeps a book of humorous quotes and thoughts out on the front desk."

"I love her!" I enthused, suddenly a very tan talk-show host.

Somehow the love got through: ten days later, Hamilton faxed me a list of twenty-four "thoughts and sayings." Included were "The second mouse gets the cheese" and the terrific "Always read stuff that will make you look good if you die in the middle of it." I asked Hamilton if it would be possible to put a specific name to four of the quotes that I liked best, including the two above; all four of the ones I picked, he told me, were the handiwork of ninety-year-old Peg Franks, a volunteer at the center. Hear her roar.

———

I KNEW there were more nuggets to be mined, but I worried that my mining method was proving to be slightly . . . haphazard. I wasn't always sure how much to trust the activities directors of senior centers when they told me they'd post my ad on their bulletin boards.

I needed to take to the streets. This decision coincided with the realization that I'd spent some seven months chasing the wisdom of old people and had not once set foot in Miami Beach. Clearly, an oversight. The high incidence of Jewish seniors in Miami make it a veritable ground zero of elder wisdom; in Hebrew, the word for old, "*zaken,*" is an acronym derived from the expression "*zeh kanah hokhmah,*" which translates as "this one has acquired wisdom."

And so I hied myself to Miami Beach for a weekend of standing on street corners and harassing fellow diners in restaurants, chatting up whichever seniors would talk to me. My first impulse, unsurprisingly, was to visit that Tabernacle of Judeo-noshing, Wolfie's Rascal House. But, sadly, the sidewalk in front of the restaurant was being repaired that weekend, which probably had much to do with the scant population of diners. (A few months later, the restaurant would close for good.) Moreover, the first diner whom I struck up a conversation with—a very pale, thin British man—immediately said, on having been apprised of my project, "A man over seventy is on the scrap heap for any woman younger than him." After lunch, I walked outside and talked to a gentleman in his nineties who lived near the restaurant; when he told me, "Don't trust politicians," I decided that the vibe at Wolfie's, aphorism-wise, was slightly off.

I had better luck on Lincoln Road, the pedestrian-clogged street in South Beach that's full of shops and restaurants. As he daubed away at a canvas that he had set up on the sidewalk, an intense, scraggly artist named Barnaby Ruhe exhorted me, "Sharpen your edges! Reset your clocks!" I wasn't exactly sure what he meant, but nevertheless I felt energized. This life-giving force was only redoubled when he said, "Sharpen your edges! Reset your clocks!" a second time; suddenly, I felt whipped up, souffléed.

About a hundred yards away from Ruhe, I sat down next to a woman named Molly Weiss, with whom I talked for a half hour. Dressed in a pink, sparkly "Rock Your Prom" T-shirt, Weiss seemed at once tightly wound and altogether relaxed. She told me, "Love is good. But sex is even better."

While I was talking with Weiss, it struck me that the task of aphorism forming is so challenging, particularly when one is asked to do it on the spot, that it might be more fruitful for me to give people the first half of an already written saying and then have them complete the saying with their own words. So I told my new friend, "You can't have enough _____," and she responded "Money!" Then I tried, "If you put a hundred people on a desert island, _____," to which she responded, "the best would survive." Then, "No, no, wait a minute—can I change my mind?" she asked anxiously as I started writing down her answer on my pad. I said sure.

"The *rest* would survive."

I told Weiss that I thought she was dark. I also said she might enjoy the work of La Rochefoucauld, a seventeenth-century duke who, after being financially ruined, stripped of his titles, and banned from Paris after the civil wars known as La Fronde, started writing witheringly pessimistic maxims like "We never praise except for profit" and "We try to make virtues out of the faults we have no wish to correct."

Weiss looked vaguely interested but then said, on a down beat, "He sounds kind of . . . French."

"That's because, in fact, he *was* French."

This did not excite her.

But the theme of the day appeared to be "French." Across from where Weiss was sitting, I found an art gallery run by a distinguished-looking eighty-five-year-old Frenchman named Michel Carel. Using his charming wife and colleague as our interpreter, I gave Carel the first half of about six sayings. He completed "You can't have enough _____" with "lovers," but then, some fifteen seconds later, he completed "The fastest way to ruin is _____" with "to find a mistress." The best minds, I thought to myself, are fraught with contradiction. As La Roche-foucauld wrote, "It is easier to appear worthy of positions one does not occupy than of those one does."

Over at the Bal Harbour mall, I chatted with two shoppers—Susan Vega and Irene Kotlowitz. Explaining to them that one of my all-time favorite aphorisms is Mohammed's "Trust in God, but tie your camel," I encouraged them to give the seventh-century saying their own ending. Kotlowitz suggested, "Trust in God, but lock your windows," and Vega said, "Trust in God, but always carry spare change for parking." I tried the same method the next day on a disheveled-looking gentleman named Arthur—no last name—and he told me, "Trust in God, but don't tell anyone what you're really thinking because if you do, they might try to hurt you or sue you, or if you live in New York City or Rio, there's a lot of guns and gang warfare there."

"I'm not sure that's a wise saying or an aphorism," I told Arthur. "It seems a little more like a rant."

"You saying I'm angry?"

"Well, yeah. Wouldn't you describe yourself that way?"

"Yeah, but I'm *good* angry."

We kept talking for a while, and Arthur offered up something of value: "You can't put the shaving cream back into the can."

I asked him if this statement reflected "a certain regretful-ness" on his part.

Arthur told me, "Story of my life."

———

WHEN I GOT BACK to New York, I had a new appreciation for how difficult it is to spin aphorisms. James Geary writes that an aphorism has four essential traits: "It must be brief," "It must be definitive," "It must be personal," and "It must have a twist." Looking through the sayings I'd assembled, I wondered how many would qualify.

And then I hit pay dirt. Deep in the bowels of a Google search one day, I came across the Web site of a seventy-five-year-old named Ashleigh Brilliant. (Yes, that's the name he was born with.) The author of such well-traveled chestnuts as "I may not be totally perfect, but parts of me are excellent" and "Support your local God," Brilliant lays claim to being history's only full-time professional published aphorist or—as Brilliant calls himself and as the Library of Congress has cataloged him— epigrammatist. Asked once by *The Wall Street Journal* whether Oscar Wilde or La Rochefoucauld didn't also qualify for such a claim, Brilliant commented, "They weren't full-time."

Born to a Jewish family in London in 1933, Brilliant started out as a painter. But people responded more to the far-out titles Brilliant gave his works than to the works themselves. Brilliant started to do pen-and-ink drawings to complement his titles, and then, before he knew it, he just started writing long lists of titles. He imposed a limit of seventeen words on his epigrams—a tribute to the number of syllables in a haiku and to the realization that he'd never used more than sixteen words anyway "but wanted a spare in case of emergencies."

Since 1975, these drawings and titles have been published under the name "Pot-Shots," appearing in newspapers and on clothing, coffee cups, and postcards. His words now appear on about a hundred million items, thus allowing Brilliant to lay claim to the title "most-quoted author."

A former Haight-Ashbury hippie and college history professor, Brilliant now lives in Santa Barbara. When I called him, he told me that, though he still writes epigrams every day, "I stopped publishing them when I hit ten thousand. I figured no one can read ten thousand epigrams. Who needs any more?"

Indeed, Brilliant's work is nothing if not the codified ramblings of a realist.

"All I want is a little more than I'll ever get."

"My life has a superb cast, but I can't figure out the plot."

"Appreciate me now and avoid the rush."

"I feel much better, now that I've given up hope."

"If you're careful enough, nothing good or bad will ever happen to you."

"In order to discover who you are, first learn who everybody else is—and you're what's left."

"Life is the only game in which the object of the game is to learn the rules."

"We owe it to our past futile sacrifices to continue making further futile sacrifices."

"Isn't there some way to get the wisdom of hindsight in advance?"

"If I can survive death, I can probably survive anything."

No aspect of Brilliant's career is more rooted in realism than the fact that he has had to protect his material—all of which is copyrighted—vigorously. In 1979, when Brilliant challenged a heat-transfer-decal company that had appropriated three of his gems, a federal judge ruled that Brilliant's works—including, in this instance, "I have abandoned my search for the truth and am now looking for a good fantasy"—were "epigrams," not "short phrases," and thus eligible for full copyright protection. He threatened to sue the Funny Side Up catalog when they emblazoned some underwear with an uncredited "I May Not Be Perfect, But Parts of Me Are Excellent." He went after Random House when David Brinkley called one of his books *Everyone Is Entitled to My Opinion*.

I asked Brilliant, "So what does it say that your profession—a profession based on revealing the truth and dispensing advice—is so fraught with legal snafus?"

He said, "My profession is based on creating a new form of literature. In order to protect it, I had to establish it as a legitimate form. The only way to do it was copyright it and take on all comers . . . You want me to relate this to wisdom, I suppose?"

"Yes, please."

"Well, the thing is, you can't be wise unless you're alive. In order to stay professionally alive, you sometimes have to protect yourself."

"And how do you respond to those people who claim that wisdom can't be self-serving?"

"Well, that's sort of like my line 'When I find true wisdom, I'll let you know (if letting you know still seems important).' I mean, maybe what you're saying is true, but who knows? I haven't found true wisdom yet. Only a wise person could answer that, and he probably wouldn't because that would be self-serving."

I asked him where his vita was headed—"What is the ideal net result of all your work?"

"You mean like never dying?"

"Maybe," I said. "Or . . ."

"What did you have in mind? Give me a multiple choice."

"I thought I read somewhere that you're hoping to win the Nobel Prize."

"Yes, my ultimate goal is the Nobel Prize."

"And how's that going?"

He had not yet received a phone call from Stockholm.

———

AFTER I'D TALKED with Brilliant, I did some more Googling and found a public lecture he gave in the spring of 2007, in a series called "What Matters Most," sponsored by the Santa Barbara City College and the Karpeles Manuscript Library Museum. At one point, Brilliant brings up the age-old query of whether we are meant to let things happen or *make* things happen—"As

Dylan Thomas put it, do you 'go gentle into that good night,' or do you 'rage, rage, against the dying of the light'?" Brilliant didn't presume to have the answer. But he did once write an epigram, he said, that he hoped people would put on their doors. The epigram read, "If I'm not home, accepting what I can't change, I'm probably out, changing what I can't accept."

This particular line of Brilliant's rang true for me because two acts I'd taken (meeting Ram Dass, scouting for aphorisms) had buoyed my spirits that were sagging after having been acted upon (being asked twice for money by Ted Bensen). Wisdom and unwisdom were always going to coexist, I now realized more than ever. I'd sated my desire to reconcile the two. And, as we know from the Buddhists, the less we want or need, the more content we are.

Or as we know from philosopher Arthur Schopenhauer, who, during the 1820s, couldn't attract a single university student to his lectures but who, some thirty years later, experienced such popular acclaim at age sixty-three due to the aphorisms in his second book that people crowded his favorite Frankfurt restaurant just to watch him eat:

> The realm of material objects is a creation, or representation, of the mind that apprehends it. The external world therefore depends on a seeing subject for its existence. The will, however, exists independently. The will—selfish, egotistical and tenacious—is also what makes life such an unpleasant business. Conflict and suffering are the only possible result in a world where billions of wills collide. Happiness, then, is not a thing in itself but merely the absence of pain; its pursuit consists in extinguishing the will, thus escaping the wretched game.

Here at the end of my search for elder wisdom, I'm surprised but delighted that, of the five traits I've come to see as being part of wisdom—reciprocity, doubt, nonattachment, discretion, and acting for social good—the one I keep running into is nonattachment. I suppose I'm heartened that it's neither doubt nor working for a social good that is the preeminent trait—the former sounds slightly psychologically crippling, and the latter physically exhausting. Discretion might be too self-abnegating. But I'm surprised it's not reciprocity.

In the end, it appears, we're alone with our demons.

Knowing what to overlook, knowing when not to fixate, extinguishing the will—I'd love to be able to call any of these skills my own. Not having them has certainly been its own toboggan ride. Man plans, and God laughs; but man fixates, and God writes and produces his own HBO comedy special.

———

I DECIDED to visit Brilliant.

Is there a more lovely place in the world to grow old than Santa Barbara? I wonder. A friendly bicycle path snakes along the beach, shaded by tall, spindly, Dr. Seussian palms; the mountain range that surrounds the city imparts a sensation that is at once comforting and bosomlike. But the best part is the air: it's tinged with eucalyptus and rosemary and pine—many big-city dwellers, if wrapped in a towel, could be convinced to pay $120 an hour just to smell it.

I met Brilliant one afternoon at his office. He's turned the small clapboard house that he and his wife used to live in into his workplace; tidy and quiet, it's filled with carousels and cardboard boxes that bear epigram-laden postcards. Working in chronological order, Brilliant has given each of his works a number from 0001 to 10,000. Walking past a carousel, I spotted 0034 ("Let's love one another, and get it over with") on a postcard and remembered that John Lennon once sent a copy of this card to Ringo Starr, writing on the flip side, "This is the truth as we see it."

We sat on the office's couch. Brilliant is wiry and bearded and was wearing shorts and black socks and black shoes; the look is errant mailman. His affect is one of determination and slight petulance; he has the facial expression of someone who is perpetually swatting at a fly.

Given that Brilliant and his wife, Dorothy, were about to celebrate their fortieth anniversary, I asked him what the secret of his marriage's success was. He reminded me that he'd once written a Pot-Shot that ran, "The secret of a happy marriage is letting people know how unhappy it is."

"And do you believe that, Ashleigh?" I asked.

"When you see our house, you'll get a better sense of what I'm talking about."

We walked about ten minutes up the gentle slope of Santa Barbara to his and his wife's house, the décor of which I would describe as Garage Sale. The floor is dotted with teetering hillocks of travel brochures that appear to have been cryogenically sealed in Ziploc bags. The furniture drifts in unconventional, slightly askew formations. Bedsheets are draped over mysterious bulges, suggesting baby elephants at rest. The paint on the ceiling and walls is peeling heavily, casting over all the mood of psoriatic unveiling.

"The reason the house is in this condition is because Dorothy owns the house," Brilliant said irritably. "I would never have it this way."

The lovely and beaming Dorothy, one hand on the couch to steady herself, raised her other hand into the air and proclaimed, "Isn't it great to own!"

I asked Dorothy what she thought the secret to her marriage's success was, and she told me, "Ignoring each other." Dorothy goes out for breakfast every day without her husband; her passion is for world travel, which she also mostly does without him.

I explained to Ashleigh and Dorothy that the paramount reason I had traveled from New York to Santa Barbara was because "I wanted to see the light switch."

A month earlier, Ashleigh had sent out a mass e-mail to his fans explaining that the light switch in his and Dorothy's dining room had stopped working two years earlier. Dorothy was unwilling either to pay an electrician or to have Ashleigh try to fix the decades-old fixture himself—Ashleigh wrote, "Dorothy takes any work on the house as personally as if it were an operation on her own body." So, for over a year, they made do with a lamp on the dining-room table instead.

But then Dorothy finally agreed to have Ashleigh try to remedy the situation. Off he went to Everything Electric, returning with a new switching apparatus. "I took it home," he wrote in his e-mail, "only to be greeted by Dorothy, as soon as she saw it, with a cry of anguish: 'It's the wrong color!' At first I didn't know what she was talking about. The whole thing was going to be buried in the back of the wall. The only part which would ever be seen was the small plastic projection which we commonly think of as the switch. But THAT, it turned out, was the part that was the wrong color."

It was white instead of ivory.

So Ashleigh returned to the store, purchased an ivory one, and went home and fixed the light.

I asked the Brilliants to show me the switch. We walked into the dining room and stared at the wholly unremarkable-looking item. I asked Dorothy what her reservations had been about having Ashleigh fix it in the first place.

"He's wonderful to say he'll try fixing it," she said, "but he has no experience as an electrician."

"She doesn't trust me," Ashleigh said, not with a surfeit of warmth.

"He could electrify himself. It's an old house. The wires are brittle. I was worried that he'd goof. Hurt himself."

We returned our gazes to the switch, like cavemen staring at fire.

I thought about its repair. I put forth, "Many men, including me, would not have gone back to the store a second time for the ivory switch. Discuss."

Dorothy rejoined, "Many men would have been artistic enough to know it needed to be a certain color."

Ashleigh blinked his eyes slowly, as if to tamp down burgeoning emotion.

I responded, "Dorothy, I'm interested that this was important to you given that the rest of the house exhibits an approach to home décor that's a little more, shall we say, laissez-faire."

"Look at that!" Ashleigh jumped in, pointing to an eighteen-inch-wide curl of paint that was peeling from the wall a few feet away.

"We couldn't do anything about that, Ash," Dorothy said. "It would cost us five thousand dollars to paint this house."

Fixing the light, by contrast, had cost $1.45.

Silence settled over us.

We trained our eyes once again on the item in question.

"I think this light switch says Something Important About Your Marriage," I said, dropping the bombshell.

· "It wasn't a big deal," Ashleigh said. "But you can make it a big deal if you want to."

I asked Ashleigh what well he had tapped into to be able to return to the store, and he said, "I realized I'd made a mistake."

We returned to staring.

Time seemed to come to a standstill.

Ashleigh shifted his weight uncomfortably from right to left. Grimace. Blink, blink. Sigh.

"OK," he finally relented, "maybe this *is* the secret of our success."

CODA

At the time of this writing, my stepfather still walks, or should I say naps, this earth.

I talk to him infrequently, but when I do, I am moved by the way he is gradually reconciling himself to my mother's departure from his day-to-day life. This cannot be easy.

After my most recent phone call with him, I was reminded of something Will said to me in 1998. I'd just published my first story in *The New Yorker*, which was probably the biggest moment of my career; I'd been rejected seven times and had finally broken through. Will, who's always been supportive of my work and who is a fan of old *New Yorker* humorists like Robert Benchley and Dorothy Parker, was thrilled for me. But in congratulating me, he said the single weirdest thing anyone has ever said to me.

We were standing in his and Mom's kitchen. I'd just come into the house bearing the issue of the magazine with my article in it. Will turned to me, congratulated me, and said, "Thank God you're gay."

"*What do you mean?*" I asked, taken aback—in the more than thirty years I'd known Will, we'd never once acknowledged my sexual orientation in front of each other, and it had nothing to do with the article.

"When I got out of college," he explained, "there were only two things I wanted to do. Write for the *New Yorker* or start a family. I did the latter, and I've wondered the rest of my life what might have happened if I'd chosen differently."

"Thank God you're gay" had struck me as being slightly deluded or egoistical—after all, there are many people who have families *and* writing careers, not to mention those who are *gay* and have families and writing careers. The genitalia you choose to consort with—outside the porn industry or Senate, of course—does not predetermine your artistic or professional trajectory.

But now I like to think that Will meant something different.

I like to think that maybe what he was really saying was, Thank God you went for it.

I like to think—even though it may sound pretentious or naïve or self-dramatizing to do so—that maybe he was somehow echoing Buddha's statement, "It is hard to live in the world and it is hard to live out of it. It is hard to be one among many." Or, as Ralph Waldo Emerson put it some 2,300 years later, "It is easy in the world to live after the world's opinion; it is easy in solitude to live after our own; but the great man is he who in the midst of the crowd keeps with perfect sweetness the independence of solitude."

I hold Will's and Buddha's and Emerson's statements close to my heart not because I think I deserve or begin to fulfill them—no, I'm too desirous of approval, and too set in my ways, to have attained Emerson's sweetness. I hold these statements close because to do so is to put all my actions under the gentle and benign stewardship of metaphor. The older I get, the more I see the need for this. But the harder it is to see.

———

I CAN SEE one thing clearly, though. I can see, one damp and gray November day, that if there is a single nugget of wisdom to be extracted from my time with the older generation, if there is one single act that all my time in the oldster trenches has prompted from me, it is this: when your mother is nice enough to let you chronicle the details of her late-in-life divorce for a reading public, you should do something nice in return for her.

And so I have decided to take Mom to the glamorous Breakers in Palm Beach for three nights, to stave off the harsh inequities of early January. I'll make no plans for the trip other than the hotel reservation—we won't be dangling over active volcanoes, and we won't be pretending I'm getting married, and we won't be chasing *Sopranos* cast members around the pool in the manner of lockjawed banshees. We'll just be hanging out and relaxing on the beach, unwinding from what has been an emotionally chaotic year.

But when the January date arrives, it is not to be, apparently. Mom's flight is delayed an hour due to bad weather. The weather in Florida is brusque and wintry—at one point, while we're walking around the hotel's premises looking at the pools it's too cold to swim in, I notice that the fierce winds are blowing Mom's cotton cover-up behind her at a ninety-degree angle. Mom chips one of her front teeth at dinner and must be persuaded not to try to Superglue it back on. The hotel management leaves a semithreatening message when other guests realize that Mom is smoking in the room. Mom finds a duvet cover that she loves at the Pratesi store—an embroidered expanse of turquoise-colored cotton and scalloped edging whose thread count threatens to burst our brain capillaries—but when the clerk tells her that it's $1,300, Mom's expression crumbles, and we scurry off empty-handed.

That night, watching TV, I turn to Mom and tell her that I feel weird writing a book about her divorce when I've never given her the full story of my breakup from my ten-year-long relationship.

"I wanna hear this," Mom says, turning off the TV.

I give her the story of how, in our eighth year, my ex and I realized we had stopped having sex and so decided to allow ourselves to see other people, as long as we did not fall in love with them. I explain that this choice, unsurprisingly, led to our demise. I explain that, despite having had my own entanglements, the fact that two of my ex's entanglements were both named Ricardo had struck me as redundant. I explain that I was less broad-minded than I hoped to be in the face of these Ricardi. I explain that I had not intended to marry the ambassador to the Latin Americas.

Over the years, I'd imagined what unburdening this story to my mother might feel like or yield, and I'd always imagined hugging or crying or perhaps a rousing duet of a showbiz standard that would be located at the intersection of Troubles I've Seen and the Danskin crotch panel.

But it does not. Mom merely nods her head sympathetically and then says she's sorry.

Talking about the breakup has been emotionally fraught for me. I go down to the hotel bar, then return to the room with a gin and tonic, realizing that it is the first time I have ever drunk alone in front of my mother.

We get talking again and Mom says, "I can't believe I've been divorced twice. People must think, She's difficult."

I counter that that's not what *I* impute to the much married. When I hear "five marriages," I don't think difficult, I think naïve. A second marriage is the triumph of hope over experi- ✓ ence, Samuel Johnson once said; so a fifth would have to be the triumph of mild dementia over hope.

Mom says, "My problem is that I'm drawn to bad boys. I know that now."

When people talk about true love, they often invoke the phrase "I'd like to grow old with that person." But the wisdom of old age might be at odds with this—maybe it's not until you're fully yourself that you can realize you've made a mistake. Maybe it's not until you've grown old that you realize you've picked the wrong person to grow old with.

———

THE NEXT DAY, we decide that we need to rise above the weather and the mood of gloom. We head over to West Palm Beach to go to the Norton Museum of Art, a small but good collection of mostly American and European nineteenth- and twentieth-century paintings. We've decided that we'll get some lunch at the museum's café and then look at art.

As we walk in from the parking lot, we pass an older couple walking toward their car. Once they're out of earshot, Mom asks me, "Was that a woman or a man?"

I tell her I wasn't sure, either, and then add, "I used to think that the three genders were male, female, and folksinger. But since I've been spending so much time with old-timers, I now realize there's also old person."

"Do I look like that?" Mom asks. She puts her arms at her sides and puffs up her chest slightly, as if on display.

"No. You're 100 percent lady," I say. "With just a touch of banana."

Once we find the café, the tide of our bad luck finally turns. The food is good, and the people-watching is even better.

Mom asks me again what I think of the divorce, and I say, sympathetically, "You did what you had to do."

I ask, "What do *you* think about it?"

She looks at me sheepishly and says, "I got in the lifeboat."

We talk a little about Will's social isolation, and Mom tells me that she's invited him to Croasdaile for a visit in a few months' time.

I say, "Interesting."

Mom explains, "I want to give him something to hope for. Not to hope that we'll get back together—he knows that's not gonna happen. But he needs something to look forward to in life." ✓

———

AFTER LUNCH, we take in the rest of the museum, marveling at the Picassos and the Vlamincks.

We waft out into the still-dark day, slightly drunk from the art, and Mom asks if I'd mind stopping at Pioneer Linens, a store she's heard about from the concierge at the hotel. I don't. I drop Mom off there and continue on by myself to look for parking. When, six minutes later, I join Mom in the store, she is already at the cash register, duvet cover in hand. She shows it to me. Its color is not the rich turquoise hue of the Pratesi. Its thread count does not cause the mind to reel or stagger. Its edges are not scalloped but, rather, crab-caked. And yet Mom shows it to me as if she were exposing me for the first time to the treasure of her newborn child. She is beaming. Here, shopping is not hope, shopping is rising above crappy circumstances, shopping is reclamation. It occurs to me that Buddha and Socrates had it easy—all they had to do to make a mark in the annals of wisdom was show up, because they were drawing the map. But the rest of us have to struggle every day to make any kind of contribution whatsoever.

"Wow, first the museum and now this!" Mom says to me excitedly as she scoops up the package, endorphins coursing through her veins like a school of tiny, silvery fish.

We push open the door of the store and walk out into the damp and unforgiving grimness of the January day. Mom announces, "I'm totally happy now." ☺

ACKNOWLEDGMENTS

I owe it all to Jon Karp. I do not speak rhetorically.

And many, many thanks to my mom and stepfather for letting me tag along during a difficult time in their lives.

Also on the honor roll: Jonathan Lazear; my main man, Greg Villepique; Jess Taylor; elder obsessive Aimée Bell; Marlo Poras; Laura Marmor and Stuart Emmrich; Nancy Graham and Ken Budd; Niloufar Motamed and Nancy Novogrod; Elissa Schappell; Rory Evans; Jenny Weisberg; Cary Goldstein; Nate Gray; Timothy Mennel; Tareth Mitch; Colin Shepherd. See you on the shuffle-board court.

ABOUT TWELVE

TWELVE

TWELVE was established in August 2005 with the objective of publishing no more than one book per month. We strive to publish the singular book, by authors who have a unique perspective and compelling authority. Works that explain our culture; that illuminate, inspire, provoke, and entertain. We seek to establish communities of conversation surrounding our books. Talented authors deserve attention not only from publishers, but from readers as well. To sell the book is only the beginning of our mission. To build avid audiences of readers who are enriched by these works—that is our ultimate purpose.

For more information about forthcoming TWELVE books, please go to www. twelvebooks.com.